TRAVEL
ESCAPADES

TRAVEL ESCAPADES

ADVENTURES AND UPSETS AROUND THE WORLD

LUKE EDWARDS

TRAVEL ESCAPADES

Copyright © Luke Edwards 2019

Second Edition 2019

Travel, Adventure, Memoire

Cover design by Sophie Lewis

ISBN 978-1-9160691-2-1

Printed and bound in the United Kingdom by IngramSpark

For Harri

We travel not to escape life, but for life not to escape us.

Anonymous

CONTENTS

Don't say you will do something tomorrow and put it off as tomorrow will never come if you use it as an excuse. If you are not currently doing it ask yourself why not. It is never too late to begin something epecially as the best day to start anything is today.

United Kingdom, 2019

PREFACE

After four years as an officer in the British Army I had yet to deploy on an operational tour. I had been based in Germany for a little over a year and taken part in a couple of month long exercises in Canada and also a number of other trips and excursions abroad, but still no deployment.

I joined the military after the British Army had left Iraq and on the eve of the withdrawal from Afghanistan. I went through training at the Royal Military Academy Sandhurst - a time when every instructor had deployed to the Middle East at least once during their career and thus our training was built upon the lessons learnt from those operations. With everyone telling their war stories I was inspired to do my bit for Queen and Country.

At the time of this book's inception my job in the Army, as a Captain, was as an Operations Officer - coordinating a fleet of vehicles and enabling the deployment of up to 120 men and women, anywhere in the world.

But one day an opportunity presented itself to me; a request came through for someone to fill a job in Somalia. Not only that but someone with my level of qualifications and experience. I immediately volunteered, sending back an email as fast as I could type the response. I then had to convince my boss to allow me to deploy - I used phrases such as "career enhancing" and "invaluable experience" to assist my argument. Ironically, as it turned out, I was the only person who had volunteered, so I was immediately given the opportunity to go overseas on my first operational tour.

Roll forward a number of months and following some specific training, with others deploying with me, I was all set to go. There soon ensued some conversation around what everyone would do in their down time whilst away, when not working. The majority of people intended to improve their fitness (or "get massive"). One of the officers said he wanted to enrol on a university short course (he never did), but I decided I would embark on the journey of writing a book, something I have always had a strong desire to undertake.

As an avid traveller, I decided to write about all the times I was travelling when things did not go quite to plan. This partially came from the desire to correct the misleading attitude arising from social media, portraying lifestyles which are unattainable for most people and also unrealistic in their flawless portrayals of places and events. These unrealistic standards have had a really negative effect on mental health for some people, so I have written this book to demonstrate that the reality of travel is often far removed from the impression some would have you believe and that despite having the best laid plans it can still go very wrong.

I hope you will enjoy my experiences with me as I take you around the world on my travel escapades, in places as diverse as Mexico and Mauritania, Nepal and Northern Europe and that you find as much amusement in my stories as I do now. Although, as I am sure you will discover, they were not particularly enjoyable at the time.

Luke Edwards,
Beledweyne, Somalia,
March 2019

SHARING THE JOURNEY

RIDING THE ORE TRAIN

Until I travelled down the length of Morocco and Western Sahara (a disputed territory, claimed by both Morocco and the self-proclaimed Sahrawi Arab Democratic Republic), I never realised quite how vast the region is. My friend Nick and I travelled from Marrakech all the way south to Dakhla on a bus; the drive was a full 24 hours, but it felt longer.

During the course of the journey we slept, both finished our books and also stopped multiple times. It took us ages to realise, as we did not speak Arabic, that most of the stops were for prayers, but some also seemed to be for tea breaks or just whenever the driver fancied it. There were also halts at random check points, which were prevalent on the outskirts of all the towns, and the dozens of bus stops along the route just for a random person to get on or off, often with a stack of luggage. It seemed like we were stopping every five minutes.

Aside from the multiple stops the journey was spectacular. For most of the time the road stayed within 100m of the sea on one side and miles and miles of desert on the other; an expanse of nothingness broken by the odd camel or cluster of sand dunes, which were welcome sights amongst the barrenness elsewhere.

Both of us were mightily relieved when we finally arrived in Dakhla. We found a place to stay, then treated ourselves to a couple of beers and a fancy(ish) restaurant, where all the locals seemed to hang out. We had an early start the following day because we needed to make the border crossing when it opened, to be able to catch a train in Mauritania later that day.

We rose before dawn for the three-hour journey from Dakhla to the Mauritanian border via taxi. Despite the early hour it was easy to find a taxi driver, but none of them were willing to take us that far out of town. They all said that we needed a Grande Taxi. A Grande Taxi turned out to be an antiquated Mercedes saloon, which was not leaving until 07:30 (because that was when the driver wanted to leave). This was an hour and a half after we had anticipated leaving and meant we would not get to the border when it opened at 09:00. We were on a pretty tight schedule, as we desperately wanted to travel on a train that left from Nouhadibou (further down the coast in Mauritania) that afternoon.

Our Grande Taxi was extremely uncomfortable for me, as I ended up in the middle seat. We had shared the fare with a Moroccan couple and the wife was in the front and I was the smallest out of the three men. To be fair, I am not sure it was much better for Nick squeezed in next to me. We stopped a couple of times en route but the remainder was spent gazing out the windows at a vast open expanse, as we headed south through the remainder of Western Sahara.

The Moroccan border check point (Western Sahara is not internationally recognised as an independent state) was quite straight forward; a stamp out of the country and a couple of forms was all it took. However, to get to the Mauritanian border control you had to travel off road for 3km through 'no-man's land,' via a rough track which was lined either side with land mines. More worrying though was a 'Mexican standoff' between the Moroccan Army (half a dozen vehicles) and the Western Saharan forces (a few vehicles and a couple of fortified gun positions) with three United Nations vehicles in the middle, just off to one side before the border. Not the ideal impression to give visitors. Nick and I surreptitiously took photos out of the window at the front lines of these two nations[1].

The Mauritanian border was much more complicated. To begin with we had to have all our details taken down and explain our itinerary to a grumpy man in a poorly lit room (there were no lights, just the sun spilling in through the door). Then we moved to another equally badly lit building, where we could actually purchase a visa. However, in that office, there was absolutely no order and people kept jumping to the front of the queue (I think Nick and I might have been the only two people queuing). It was painful to watch as the man scanning passports appeared to take them at random from the pile on his desk. We eventually won the lucky dip and were served. Our finger prints were taken, as well as a photo for our visas. This was a completely arbitrary process, as in mine I was looking down at the time the picture was taken, so I looked asleep. Then I had a code printed over my face, so you could hardly see it anyway.

After this drawn out process, our passports were handed on to another guy who stuck the visas in and charged a whopping €120 for doing

---

[1] These photos were later asked for by a friend of a friend who worked at the British Foreign and Commonwealth Office (FCO).

it. This turned out to be one of the most expensive visas in the world at the time, although it has since been halved in price. Whilst struggling to jump through all these hoops we met our first fellow English traveller, who was a plumber from Essex and owned a house in Gambia. He was driving down the West Coast, taking a similar route to us and staying in Gambia (one of the five English speaking countries in West Africa) for the winter. After all that rigmarole we had to go to a third and final building, where they asked more questions and then finally stamped the visas, permitting us entry to the country.

Once inside Mauritania it was not plain sailing either, as every few hundred metres there were check points. Here our car was pulled over and we had to hand over our passports or, on a couple of occasions, we had to write down our details.

Despite our best endeavours, we had been slowed up so much at the border with the bureaucracy and inefficiency of the officials, that about 10km outside Nouhadibou we saw our train, having left on time from the station, heading towards us in the opposite direction, on the track that runs alongside the road. Not wanting to give up on our plan, we walked to the station anyway to enquire about the next train. We were told it departed between three and four that afternoon, which suited us perfectly as we needed to buy food and water for the 12-hour journey across the desert.

We bought loaves of bread, a lot of water and some Nutella for sustenance on the journey (the only ingredients needed for a solid diet[2]). We then had great hilarity with currency, as we had exchanged money at the Moroccan border and had no idea what the value of a Mauritanian Ouguiya was worth, or how to pronounce it.

We returned to the train station just after 3pm, but had to wait until 5pm for the train to actually arrive. During the wait we were greeted by a very friendly customs officer, who spoke excellent English and told us we were very welcome in his country and it was not often that they had visitors from England. This was hardly surprising as neither Nick or I knew of anybody else who had travelled there (and to this day I still do not).

The next leg of our journey was on a two and a half kilometre long iron ore train, which is one of the longest trains in the world. We were catching it from the port in Nouhadibou and travelling overnight for 12 hours into the Saharan

---

[2] Not actual weight loss or healthy living advice.

Desert in one of the empty ore carriages. Most locals (and the occasional tourist who ventures that far) sit inside one of the passenger coaches at the rear. If you're on a tighter budget there is a less comfortable but still legal option of riding in the carts. We had read a few snippets online from a couple of other travellers, but nothing could have prepared us for the epic journey.

When the huge diesel locomotive pulled into the station we madly ran along to the end of the platform and along beside the rails to an empty truck, where we clambered aboard with our rucksacks. We need not have hurried so much, as there were three men laboriously loading a herd of goats into one cart, further down the train. A short time later we slowly pulled out of the station; the excitement was hard to hide from our faces.

Trundling through the desert with dust and iron ore flying in our faces, seeing the vast expanse of the desert was unbelievable. We had Shemaghs (traditional Middle Eastern head-scarves) wrapped tightly around our faces. I also had sunglasses to shield my eyes. although the ski goggles Nick had brought to wear were definitely more effective. Every direction you looked there was sand to the horizon. We stood leaning over the edge of the carriage, gazing out into the empty space, lost in our thoughts as the train rumbled on, its clatters the only sound we could hear.

The train continued to rattle through the evening across a vast flatness and we watched in awe as the sun touch the horizon, throwing out incredible shades of orange and pink, before it dipped lower and briefly enveloped everything in a burst of the deepest red, before disappearing for the night. The darkness then surrounded us.

With no majestic scenery to keep us occupied, we tucked into our loaves of bread and chocolate spread scooped out in massive lumps, washing the grittiness of the desert away with swishes of water. With not much else to do, we rolled out our carpets, which we had bought in Marrakech, laid down and gazed up at the clearest sky either of us had ever seen, whilst chatting and putting the world to rights. This was undoubtedly the coolest thing either of us had ever done. It is safe to say that the train journey lived up to our expectations.

With the sun long gone and the residual heat having vanished, it quickly became very cold. We had not-so-cleverly undertaken this trip in December, not a month renowned for being the warmest of the year in the Northern Hemisphere. We were also in a desert, which notoriously gets cold at night; combine those two with the fact we were in an enormous iron box and it felt as if we were lying in a huge fridge. Even though we had trousers (I had tucked mine into my socks by this point), t-shirts, shirts, jumpers, djellabas (Moroccan National Dress which are woollen robes with hoods), woolly hats and we had now rolled ourselves in our rugs, we were still cold.

There were definitely times when I questioned what we were doing. Even on the odd occasion when I might have been dropping off to sleep, the train would slow down just a fraction and every cart would bang into the one ahead. You could hear this start way off in the distance and as it reached the carriages closest to us it would get louder, right up to the point where ours would crash into the one in front. Then, almost immediately, the train would speed up a fraction and the same thing would happen again in reverse. Towards the end of the night we could work out the exact moment our cart would collide with a neighbouring one just by listening to the clangs coming down the line. I have certainly had more restful nights, but I still maintain its enjoyability.

We arrived in Choum (a small town in the middle of nowhere) at 02:30 and we wandered around in the dark for a little while, until we were kindly pointed to the 'taxi office' where about 20 men were arguing over space and luggage on the back of a Toyota pickup truck. Like them we too wanted to go to Atar, another desert town, three hours away across the sand. We were too late to the party but were told another truck should arrive within the next hour. Neither of us had managed to get any sleep on the train, due to the noise and cold, so we both pulled out our rugs again and tried as best as we could to get comfortable against a wall and waited.

Unfortunately for us the bus did not turn up until 10:00, much later in the day than we had hoped. To make matters worse, I had still not managed to sleep and a litre and a half of water had emptied itself in my rucksack; the bottle must have split when I launched my bag over the edge of the train when we disembarked. Not a great start to the day.

The pickup was a flatbed, loaded with bags and bundles. There were so many pieces of luggage that they came well above the level of the cargo bed and had to be tied and strapped down with a large net. On top of this mountain of baggage sat 13 men, including me and Nick.

As we had not understood a shouting man telling us that we were finally ready to leave, we were slow off the mark and consequently were the last two to clamber aboard. We were left with the worst seats right on the edge and were only able to hold on with our fingers looped through the gaps in net. We spent the next two and a half hours clinging on for our lives; every bump sent us swaying, each time nearly unseating us. The first half of the journey was all off road, following small tracks through the sand. Every bounce felt as if it would send us flying off the truck. I even had a nice local holding onto my shoulder, in an attempt to help me not meet my maker.

The second half was on a metalled road, which if anything was scarier, as the driver drove flat out, at over 70 mph. Both of us were still struggling to stay on and had our legs hanging over the side, watching the ground rush past. We stopped at a handful of check points; some looked military run, but others looked more like a ragtag bunch of militiamen. All of them wanted to see our passports, but we were always let through without much hassle; the locals we shared the ride with made sure of that. The one time when we were asked to go into a hut, two of the guys jumped off the back of the truck and came with us to make sure we were OK, a touching act of kindness.

When we finally slowed down upon entering the town of Atar we were both glad to hop off and shake out the strain in our arms. We also both agreed that the journey on the truck was probably more enjoyable than the train, but we decided they were two equally exciting modes of transport.

Atar had promised to be a gateway into the desert, with a number of tour operators running their outfits from there, as well as a flourishing artisan trade selling silver objects. We hunted high and low for any evidence of either, but both were impossible to track down, despite searching the whole centre of town. Clearly in the not too distant past there had been a greater flow of tourist traffic and the silversmiths and tour operators would have been easier to find.

We had not seen any other travellers since leaving the border. At the time that we visited, the Foreign and Commonwealth Office (FCO) advised against all travel to the region on account of the Islamist militant groups, who had freedom of movement throughout the Sahara Desert. It was a huge shame as both of us agreed that Mauritania was one of the most beautiful countries we had ever been to and the people we met were almost certainly the friendliest. Not once did we feel unsafe and it should definitely be on people's wish list (security situation permitting)[3].

For lunch we found a small restaurant, which we originally thought was someone's house. It might actually have been someone's house, but they were enterprising and offered us food and we had a lovely meal of spicy fish and rice. Instead of hanging around in Atar, where there was nothing happening, we carried on along the road for another six hours, passing through yet more breath-taking scenery, to the capital Nouakchott.

Here we made our way, via taxi, to the bus 'terminal' for transport to the Mauritanian/Senegalese border. After paying and then waiting for about 45 minutes we set off in a rather cramped minibus on a six-hour journey through the countryside. The two of us were in the front seats, so had great views of the endless sand for the first half of the drive and then gradually saw the change of landscape, as it became greener, the further south we headed.

The border town of Rosso was like any other transitory town: busy, noisy, dirty and full of people after your money. As we had both done

---

[3] Please refer to FCO guidance, North Africa can be a volatile region and the security situation changes frequently.

many border crossings around the world, we felt confident that we would not fall foul of any of the local's tricks to get us to pay for extra things.

We initially had to take a horse and cart (yes you read that correctly) from the bus stop to the frontier; these were the only taxis available. The border town was a few kilometres away and when we arrived there were half a dozen men surrounding us, before we had even jumped down. All of them were shouting and telling us they would help us if we gave them our passports and a certain amount of money.

Feeling certain that we could manage the border and negotiate the various stages fine by ourselves, without the need to pay someone, we walked up to one of the border guards. Unfortunately, all the border officials were in on a huge scam and probably took a cut from the money made. When we spoke to the guard, he asked to see our passports, before we could go through the gate to the border offices, which we felt was reasonable. However, after inspecting them they were handed over to one of the men who had been following us. We were quite frankly furious, we had tried our hardest not to be caught out, but we had been let down by a corrupt official. As far as we could see there was no way of beating the system, without spending hours arguing about it (we spent a good ten minutes without getting anywhere).

In order to get stamped out of the country and to retrieve our passports, we were firstly directed to a dingy shop to make a copy of our passport and to change some money (at a very poor rate) for the ferry (the border was on the Senegal River).

The 'helper' still would not return our passports, but walked to passport control to have them stamped for us. The guard in there dutifully stamped us out of Mauritania, but then agreed with our 'helper' that we had to pay $15 each for the privilege of the stamp and the ferry ticket (which was marked up as the equivalent of 30p). This was nothing but extortion and my blood was boiling. Nick attempted to sort the situation by making a grab for the passports. His failed attempt resulted in a very heated argument in a mixture of French and English, drawing a large crowd of our helper's friends. Just before Nick was beaten up and lynched, I fished in my pocket for the money and very begrudgingly handed over $30. Thankfully it did mean the safe release of our passports. Fuming, we walked away to the ferry terminal muttering our most choice phrases under our breaths.

At the water front we were informed that the ferry was not leaving for another three hours, but we could pay $5 to go across on a water taxi (the tickets we had been forced to buy were just valid on the car ferry, which only left a couple of times a day). More arguing got us nowhere and wanting to get away from the whole situation as quickly as we could, we boarded a water taxi and crossed the river. We shared the ride with a Senegalese man who was friendly and had tried to help us negotiate a price.

On the Senegalese side we were suspicious of everyone, after our recent experience on the northern side of the river, but there really was not much of an issue. We even managed to exchange money at a reasonable rate with our new Senegalese friend; he actually helped with fending off touts and other hustlers. Once we had exchanged a suitable quantity of money, he took us away from the main river crossing area, along the road, to the travel depot.

At the transport hub there were two options to travel to Dakar (the capital of Senegal): either a minibus, which would stop frequently and we would have to wait until it was completely full, something which could take anywhere between half an hour and half a day; or we could go in a Sept-Place (seven-seater, although more commonly an eight or nine-seater) which would go direct and cost a little more. We chose the latter and were given two of the three seats in the boot of an ancient five-seater Peugeot estate. The other space in the boot was taken by a Mauritanian man and his small nephew; the nephew sat on his lap. The man was in the Mauritanian Navy and in the fortunate position that he could afford to take his nephew to Dakar for medical treatment. He freely admitted that healthcare in Mauritania was not up to scratch, hence why he was travelling all the way to the Senegalese capital. In the boot it was an impossibly tight squeeze, in a very hot car, making the whole journey extremely uncomfortable.

The journey from the border to Dakar should have taken around six hours, but because the car was so old (it literally had dozens of rust holes in the roof and doors) it took considerably longer, with plenty of stops added in to refill the coolant which was leaking. Just as it was getting dark, we pulled up at a non-descript petrol station, in some random town, about 60km outside Dakar. The driver turned around and informed us that he would not drive any further. He refused to carry on, even though all seven of us had paid the full price to travel all the way to Dakar. The whole car erupted in shouting and gesticulations; Nick and I joined in with the complaining once we understood what was going on.

Thankfully our Mauritanian friend spoke very good English and was also bold enough to fetch the police; we had stopped opposite a police station (not the driver's smartest move). Despite the police's involvement, the driver still refused to drive any further, so the police made him pay for everyone to get other taxis to Dakar.

The three of us and the nephew stuck together, because our friend knew that we needed his help with the language barrier and because we were white tourists and therefore more likely to be scammed or ripped off on the price. Eventually after an hour of waiting we were in a different taxi on our way again. We paid the driver a little extra and he took us to our hostel. After our border experience I had lost faith in Mauritanian people, but the Naval Officer fully restored it and then some.

Our hotel was pretty central and the cheapest we could find. It was not amazing, but at after midnight we were not in too much of a position to complain and search elsewhere. One of the owners spoke English and after showing us the room took us to an ATM, which supposedly had the best exchange rate for English cards in the city.

A beer was next on the agenda (something we had been promising ourselves all day) so we made our way to a bar recommended by the hotel owner. About 30 seconds after we had ordered our beers it was clear why he had taken us to that particular establishment. Two young, local girls came over and introduced themselves. They were not impressed when we said we were not interested, but they still stayed around, trying to engage us in conversation. It made the whole situation very uncomfortable; we had just wanted to grab a drink and chill, but under the circumstances it had not been relaxing at all. We hurriedly finished our drinks and left as soon as we could, in order to find some food and get some much-needed rest.

The day had the potential to be a brilliantly exciting day of travel, with one of the coolest border crossings I had ever done, but instead it was full of arguments, let downs and completely unnecessary stress and bureaucracy. I cannot remember a worse day of travelling.

ROAD TRIP TO RUIN

Chris, my friend of about ten years, and I decided to undertake a road trip around Europe in my recently purchased 13-year-old Volvo estate car. I had bought it because I was moving to Germany with the Army. I required a car that was suitable for driving long distances, but also one that had the capacity to carry a lot of luggage; the Volvo ticked both boxes.

The plan was to drive around all the micronations in Europe, the tiny countries nobody usually visits, unless by accident, and Chris was coerced into joining me for the journey. We decided on a route which would take us through France, Belgium, Luxembourg, Germany, Switzerland, Liechtenstein, Italy, San Marino, Monaco, Spain, Andorra and back home to the UK via France. It would be roughly 2,500 miles of driving, spread over six days. We would sleep in the back of the car, as the seats folded down flat, in order to save some money and we had the flexibility of having our own transport to stop and explore places when we fancied.

The journey started very early on a Saturday morning. I loaded my bags into the cavernous boot of the estate and drove around the corner from my house to pick up Chris. He piled out of his parents' home wearing shorts, Aviators and a straw hat; arguably attire more suited to a Caribbean beach holiday than wandering around some of Europe's finest capital cities.

Once we were all packed, we set off towards Calais. A couple of hours later we had checked in, driven onto the Eurotunnel, spent half an hour on the train under the English Channel and were emerging into France with the first light of day. Free movement of people within the Schengen Area[4] would allow us to drive across borders as if Europe was one large country. To the sound of 'Bitter Sweet Symphony' we pulled out of the train, up the ramp and onto the motorway.

Having driven out of Calais and left all remnants of the coast behind, it was not long before we were driving across Belgian soil. Renowned worldwide for its chocolate, we were

---

[4] An area of 26 European countries which have open borders with each other, i.e. no requirement for passport checks.

tempted to make a pitstop for some, but felt we could not justify the extra calories on top of the half-dozen French pastries we had already eaten that morning, especially as it was not yet even eight. Reluctantly we decided to drive straight through to Luxembourg.

The car was too old to have a built-in satnav and we did not want to pay for roaming charges to use Google Maps (the days before you could use data for free in Europe). Being young and poor we did not even have a satnav you could plug into the cigarette lighter, so we were resorting to the tried and tested method of using a road atlas to navigate our way; with its use it brought back memories of my childhood.

This old school navigation technique resulted in us missing a turning off the motorway around the outskirts of Brussels. This minor navigational error left us heading towards the city centre. By the time Chris and I realised we were not travelling on the road we should have been it was too late. Our road atlas, with a scale of 1-900K, did not have a detailed map of Brussels so we were in no place to pick our way out of the mess, instead we resorted to using a compass bearing (Scout and military training coming in handy) and ploughing straight through the heart of the city. We hoped that using this method we would eventually hit the ring road on the other side of the capital.

I had slightly more faith in the idea than Chris, but then again it was me who suggested it, so naturally I had to back my own plan. The impromptu city tour added about an hour onto our journey time and was one of the most traumatic driving experiences of my life. There were so many traffic lights and one-way streets, as well as pedestrian crossings and tram routes. Driving on the wrong side of the road, whilst attempting to cross two queues of solid traffic to reach the correct lane for a turning was a nightmare. The Volvo was built for cruising at 70 mph on the motorway, not driving around picturesque streets in a city. After that fiasco we made sure we were much more careful when looking for signs.

Eventually we made it to the ring road and then on to Luxembourg. When we arrived we found a parking space towards the outskirts of Luxembourg City and meandered our way towards the centre of the capital, passing through a well-manicured public garden and interesting architecture. The buildings seemed to me to be a mixture of steep German roofs sat atop tradition- al Renaissance style French buildings. Regretta- bly we had to back-track to the car, just as we had reached the main square, because I suddenly realised that I had not locked the car. It was the first day on the road, so mistakes were always going to happen, but Chris was less than impressed with my actions.

Having trekked back into the centre we visited the royal residence and then settled down at a café on the square for a coffee and a few hands of cards. At least we thought it was a café until the moment we saw silver platters with lobster, crab and oysters served to a table of two well-dressed couples on the table next to us.

It is rare that I feel awkward when travelling, but I certainly felt out of place and vastly under-dressed sat there in my shorts, t-shirts and flip flops. We finished our game, paid and sauntered off, trying to emit the air of people who frequently dine at high-end establishments.

After taking some obligatory tourist pictures we returned to the car and hit the road again. This time we drove into Germany, our fifth country of the day. Both Chris and I had previously visited Germany on a number of occasions, so we were not too desperate to stop anywhere to see the sights. However, we were keen to see the speed of the autobahns and therefore we used Germany as a transit country to Switzerland, instead of France (the autobahns are far quicker than French motorways.) The Volvo was built for driving long distances on motorways, so the cruise control was utilised, the tunes turned up and great conversation flowed.

After belting our way south through the flatlands of north Germany, we finally reached some hills, which indicated the start of the Bavarian mountains. During the hours we were on the autobahns we put the world to rights, decided that any Taylor Swift album is a worthy addition to a road trip compilation and concluded that the Italians are the most aggressive drivers in Europe. After nearly 600 miles behind the wheel I pulled into a service station somewhere in Bavaria, where we grabbed some cheap food and stayed the night.

The following day, after many hours on the road, listening to a whole plethora of music, we reached Switzerland; the land of watches, mountains and chocolate, (the rivalry between Swiss and Belgium chocolate makers is fierce). The roads we drove along were small and wound their way through the mountains, shrouded in shadows. The peaks soared far above us, still covered in the winter snow. I was content to be stuck behind a lorry for some of the time because it gave me, as the driver, an opportunity to look at the insanely beautiful country we were passing through.

Finally, we reached Zurich, where we parked the car and went exploring. We did not get far before we wandered down one of the main shopping streets. Every building was occupied by a designer brand (all far beyond our price bracket) and the pavement was made of marble slabs.

Feeling out of place once again we noticed there were a couple of fancy looking churches nearby; the Fraumunster Church with impressive stained-glass windows and St Peter's Church, which has the largest clock face in Europe. Even though both were remarkable they were nothing compared to the incredible views we had witnessed whilst driving through the rest of the country. Switzerland is honestly worth a visit, just for driving the roads (even in an estate car).

We briefly left Switzerland to visit its tiny neighbour Liechtenstein, a double land locked country[5]. Nestled amongst Alpine peaks, the miniature capital Vaduz has neither an airport nor a train station and its tourist attractions were

---

[5] A country which is surrounded by other landlocked countries, there are only two double landlocked countries in the world, Uzbekistan is the other.

unsurprisingly not in the same league as the Eifel Tower or the Houses of Parliament.

Vaduz city centre is not on most people's holiday itinerary, as there are not a lot of things to do there; you can walk through the city in a matter of minutes (we quickly proved this theory). Despite trying to prolong our stay by visiting the stamp museum and Vaduz Castle, the principle landmark that can be seen from virtually every point in the city (it is perched atop a cliff), we still did not stay more than two hours.

Back in the car we wove our way south through more of beautiful Switzerland, over the Alps and on into Italy (yet another new country for me). We drove over numerous mountain passes, dozens of bridges and through so many tunnels we lost count. I turned up "On days like these", the theme tune for the Italian Job and it felt like we were on set.

Fortunately, unlike in the film, we did not come across bulldozers at the end of any of the tunnels en route. It was already well into the afternoon when we crossed the border, so we decided we would go to Milan (the nearest city) for dinner. Naturally we did a bit of sightseeing, the highlight being the Cathedral, which is the fifth largest church in the world. Unfortunately, it was closed, so we were unable to go inside, but even so it was pleasant to have as a backdrop as we ate pizza at a street-side café.

The pizza was good, but the service was slow and we were served by a very rude waitress. Perhaps she was cross the church was closed too, or maybe it was because we had chosen to eat at such an early hour - 18:30 instead of the usual 23:00 like the locals. Either way we were not too disappointed to pay and return to the car. After half an hour of more driving, we reached some services, where we dropped the back seats down, unravelled our roll mats and sleeping bags and settled down for our second night on the road.

The following morning, we had a decision to make: either to drive 350 kilometres in the wrong direction to visit the micro nation San Marino, or save time and head towards France. I decided we could afford the day's driving to visit such a unique country and I managed to convinced Chris that he would otherwise probably never see it in his life. Most people, outside of Europe, have probably never even heard of the country and most Europeans have probably only heard of the country because of their abysmal footballing legacy (they have only won one game in the country's history) or their equally successful attempts at the Eurovision Song Contest.

The small country is completely surrounded by Italy and claims to be the oldest surviving sovereign state in the world. Anyone who has visited the hilltop nation will understand why it has never been invaded successfully. Atop the imposing rock pinnacle is a fortress, which provides views to the Adriatic Sea in the East and as far as the eye can see in the West. Although only a small country, which would only ever have been defended by a few hundred men, I think it is clear to see why the Italians never conquered the Sammarinese[6]. To reach it the Volvo laboured its way up the steep incline to the fortress. I can only imagine how tough it would have been to fight your way up the hill in medieval armour; rather them than me.

We did not stay there long, but were able to see the whole city in a couple of hours, so felt we did not require more time. The steep cobblestoned streets were fun to explore and we wandered around until we had visited everything that was considered a 'tourist attraction'. These included: the parliament (which was housed in an old guard tower), Liberty Square (a drinking fountain with a statue above it) and of course, the

---

[6] Citizens and people of the country of San Marino.

famous fortress which sits right at the top of the hill.

Despite it being an independent sovereign nation, San Marino felt very similar to Italy, especially the local cuisine. However, when I told the chef, at the little restaurant we picked for lunch, that his pizzas were so good that they tasted like real Italian ones, he did not take it as a compliment!

We drove back the same way we had arrived into San Marino, then west through Northern Italy, again through stunning scenery, before a short drive through Southern France. We chose the delightfully pretty coastal road, which had excellent views out to sea and many bends, which the Volvo took in its stride like any grand tourer. On arrival and after parking the car in Monte Carlo (the capital of Monaco), we decided to pay homage to the casino, one of the most famous in the world.

I knew I could not travel all this way without having at least one spin on the roulette (I would have sat and played cards all day had we not been on a tight schedule). However, like all great plans ours was thwarted at the first hurdle. The security guard would not let Chris in with shorts, flip flops and a t-shirt. After going back to the car to change we returned 15 minutes later and were both allowed to enter the famous establishment.

I am not usually a gambler but visiting such an iconic location would not be complete without having a little wager. I nervously placed €50 on red and waited until all other bets had been placed and the ball was in the croupier's hand. Anyone who has ever played roulette will know the feeling of suspense as the croupier places the small ball inside the circular track, spins the wheel and then launches the ball around in the opposite direction. The brief moment where everything is in motion and there is nobody who can change the outcome; everyone is watching the wheel, breaths held. Then the whole thing starts slowing down, the ball drops down out of the track, bounces a few times, hops from number to number, still not sure where it wants to come to rest, before finally coming to a halt in one of the pockets. I saw it was sat in Red 19.

I was over the moon and not being flush with cash, I quit whilst ahead, leaving with double the money with which I had entered; enough to top up the car and get a couple of beers to celebrate.

Monte Carlo was the first, and only, city on our road trip on a sea coast and we agreed that no holiday is complete without a dip in the ocean.

Despite feeling we had to swim in the sea, neither of us felt very enthusiastic after we felt the temperature of the water. A middle-aged lady who was swimming lengths across part of the harbour made us feel that we had to get in for at least a brief dip, if only to maintain our pride. After many gasps and splutters we were both in the water, swimming madly around to try and warm up, but to no avail. About ten minutes later we were back on dry ground, frantically putting our clothes on over our damp bodies. Whatever anyone ever tries to tell you, I can assure you that the Mediterranean really is not that warm in April.

We had a casual walk around the harbour, admiring the super yachts, whilst playing a game of trying to guess their owner's profession, wondering how much each would cost and coming up with inventive ideas of how we could get ourselves invited on board. We decided we would first have to buy new clothes before any of the owners would even speak to us.

Once back in the car we drove out of the city, along some of the Formula One race track, as they had already laid the new surface for the following weekend's race. The home straight was one of the areas which they had already tarmacked and they had built the grandstand, which made the little boy inside me smile with delight, even though we were driving at 30kmph. Having driven on a variety of different quality roads so far on this trip, this was like driving on grippy marble, it was so flat and smooth. Arguably my most pleasurable driving experience ever.

We made a dash out of Monaco and along the French coast down to Spain. We had not initially intended to visit Spain, as it is a country both of us had visited a number of times before, but again the map let us down and we drove past the correct turning for Andorra and we were driving over the international boundary before we realised our mistake. We turned around at the next junction and made the correct turning into the last micro nation of our journey.

Andorra is nestled high in the Pyrenees; we had to drive up a winding mountain pass, flanked by a number of snow-covered peaks, whilst envying the people skiing down the slopes, as we drove on up to the capital, Andorra La Vella; a small, uninteresting place which happens to be the highest city in Europe.

Feeling hungry, but with no money for food, I walked to the nearest ATM and went to withdraw some money, only to find that when I looked in my wallet, I had lost my bank card. It was in the days before I had any credit cards, so I had no other options. I remembered that Chris had talked about having brought an international currency card, so I gave him a shout to come over and withdraw some money, only for him to utter the crushing words of "I don't have any money on it". It transpired that Chris had assumed I would have the financial side of the trip sorted and he would only need to use his card in an emergency. He had not even brought his debit card with him. When I explained this was an emergency, because we had no way of buying food or fuel, the penny dropped.

He then tried to load his international currency card with money, using free Wi-Fi, but either the internet or his phone could not handle the situation and it failed to work. We even phoned his mum to try and load the card from a computer in England but this too failed. Disheartened and struggling to find a solution to the problem, we concluded that I must have left my bank card at a petrol station way back in France, a few hundred kilometres ago, where we had last filled up. We also worked out that we probably did not have enough money or fuel to get back there. My genius plan was to try and make it to Barcelona, where there was a British Consulate who would hopefully loan us some money; although we were not 100 percent sure that was the sort of thing they did. I checked they were open that day and went back to the car.

At the Volvo, just before we set off for Barcelona, I suddenly had a realisation that I was now wearing jeans, as it was cold in the mountains, whereas earlier I had been wearing shorts. I sheepishly rummaged in the pockets of my shorts and lo and behold I found my card in the back pocket. Nearly an hour wasted worrying over a stupid mistake; it was a couple of lessons learned. It was a great relief to be able to buy some food and make full use of the cheap fuel. We decided to leave Barcelona for another trip.

When we attempted to leave Andorra, we were pulled over and asked to explain why we had stayed for only one day. We regaled our story, but the border guard did not find it as amusing as we did. We were then questioned about smuggling and asked how many cigarettes and how much alcohol we had bought; our response of "none" brought high levels of suspicion so we had to open the boot and remove all our belongings. A brief search with a sniffer dog confirmed our story and we were allowed on our way, back down, out of the mountains and into warmer climes.

I have visited France on dozens of occasions. Every summer, whilst growing up, I spent two weeks camping all over France's numerous regions. During the course of the different holidays I travelled using a huge array of transport, including: canoeing down the Loire, crossing the country via coach and train, using Paris' subway system, cycling in the summer sun to the beach. I have even hitch hiked in Corsica, but none of these previous trips would match what we were about to encounter.

Having just filled up with cheap fuel in Andorra (€0.99 per Litre of diesel [2015]) we were on the home stretch. We were cruising along the motorway, tunes blaring away, basking in the Friday afternoon sun, when the Volvo started playing up. I am not going to pretend I am a car expert, but when the turbo kept jumping, subsequently over-revving the engine, I knew something was not quite right. It may have something to do with the fact we had been averaging about 500 miles a day over the previous four days or it could have just been that the old girl was wearing out.

I decided to press on, albeit slightly slower, in the hopes of nursing the car home and taking it to a garage once back in England. Unfortunately, we never made it. In fact, we were not even close. We stopped virtually half way between Montauban and Brive (which for those of you whose French geography is not quite up to scratch, in layman's terms it was in the South of France). It was half seven in the evening when we pulled onto the hard shoulder and used the emergency phone.

Attempting to talk to the mechanic was a struggle, as his English was worse than our French (which was saying something). We eventually managed to explain where we were and understood that he was coming to get us. When he arrived the language barrier was even worse, but all was not lost as thankfully I have a sister who is fluent in French and has even lived there, so I called her and then passed my phone to the mechanic. She was very handy and acted as a translator, but later admitted that even she struggled with his local dialect and slang terminology, especially when he started getting technical about the car.

We had a pressing issue due to the fact that all the garages were now shut for the evening and would not be opening again until Monday (the French do not work weekends at all). Unfortunately for us, I needed to be back in work on Monday for the last two weeks of a four-month course and then I was flying to Canada for two months and therefore could not hang around.

After the estate had been hauled onto the back of a recovery truck, in the failing light, we both jumped into the front of the cab and drove to the garage he had come from. We tried to make small talk with our GCSE French as we pulled off the motorway and on through small French towns, but the conversation did not last long; it turned out that he did not play football with his brother.

At the garage the car was unloaded and we entered an office where I rang my sister to translate again. The outcome was that we would have to leave our keys and pick the car up on Tuesday or Wednesday, as the work would take two days at least, not exactly ideal. After some negotiating, the keys were returned to me "so I could get some things out of the car" because in "no way [were we] allowed to sleep on the forecourt overnight." However, we had no other option than to stay overnight in the car as the sleepy village had nowhere to stay, nowhere to eat and no form of running transport (the next bus was at 11:00 the following morning). After the owner and mechanic had left, we unrolled our sleeping mats and bags and climbed into the back of the Volvo.

One of my favourite things about travelling is working out problems and finding the best solution, so I was quite enjoying this addition to our adventure; Chris however was not. Mobile reception at the garage was poor to say the least and not good enough to use roaming data, but both of us had sent numerous messages back to people in the UK, to help us search for the nearest/cheapest/easiest way of returning home. Amazingly, it turned out that some family friends lived just 20 miles away and they were willing to help us out. This news definitely brightened the atmosphere.

The following morning, not long after dawn, we were picked up by the family friend I had not seen in eight years. I was surprised she recognised me, although there could not have been many young Englishmen waiting at the side of the road that early in the morning. Whilst we caught up about the intervening years, she drove us to the largest nearby town, Brive. There we were able to buy tickets for a number of trains throughout the day and overnight to Paris, where we arrived after many games of cards and little sleep.

We jumped on a Eurostar early on Sunday morning, which took us back to London and then home. The road trip did not turn out to be quite as cheap as we had anticipated, due to the train fares and me forking out for the expensive recovery and repairs, but we saw all the micronations that we had intended to visit, had a great laugh in the car and ended up with a more exciting journey than we could have imagined.

Back in the UK, I had the problem of retrieving the car. I had returned to work and it would have been two weeks before I was free to pick it up; the garage said they would charge €20 a day to keep it there. It sounded like it would be an expensive carpark.

Thankfully my Dad offered to take a couple of days off work to collect the car and also to visit the family friends. He actually sounded really enthusiastic about the impromptu holiday. Unfortunately, the car failed to make it all the way back on that occasion too; the problem had not been correctly fixed, so the Volvo broke down again just 40 miles away from the garage. A one-night trip turned into three, before the car finally limped its way back to old Blighty. I think it is safe to say that I owed my dad.

GUINEA VISA WOES

Anyone who has travelled will appreciate that plans quite often do not go as expected. Anyone who has travelled in Africa will also know that on the odd occasion that things do go to plan, they may go far slower than anticipated. Nick (a friend of mine from work) and I travelled around the West Coast of Africa overland. We were trying to work our way from Gambia to Sierra Leone, travelling through Senegal, Guinea-Bissau and Guinea.

Gambia is a former colony of the United Kingdom and as such the country spoke English. When we visited, we stayed in a terrible hotel (by terrible I mean with no hot water or WiFi) in Banjul, having arrived by ferry a couple of hours before. We visited the imaginatively named Arch 22 and with that we had exhausted the city of all its sights (there was really only one). The arch had been constructed by the President as a memorial to him taking over power in the form of a coup on 22nd July 1994. He was still President over 20 years later when we visited.

The following day we decided to rise early as we knew we had a long day ahead of us, since we needed to travel from Banjul in Gambia, through a small section of Senegal, (as the country surrounds Gambia) and then on to Bissau, the capital of Guinea-Bissau.

Nick and I flagged down a minibus, the main form of transport for locals, and clambered on with our luggage. Our fellow passengers threw us some dirty looks and some of them were not too impressed with our bags. We were reluctant to put them on the roof, with everyone else's belongings, for the fear of something being stolen and they were both small enough to be considered hand luggage on a plane, so we put them at our feet. This unfortunately further limited the already sparse leg room.

The minibus took us an hour south of Banjul to the town of Brikama, the main transport hub for the region. There we hoped we would be able to catch some onward transport fairly easily.

The Sept-Place we travelled in on that day was the smallest one we had yet to have the 'pleasure' of occupying. It was so tiny that Nick was not even able to sit up properly in the back, as he was too tall; even for me at 5' 8" it felt rather cramped with modest headroom available. We were stuck in the 'boot' where a bench seat had been placed and had the auspicious pleasure of sharing it with a rather large lady. Unfortunately, she had plonked herself down and occupied the third and final seat and also occupied most of my third of the bench. This added discomfort made the three-hour journey to Ziguinchor, the nearest town to the border, fairly unpleasant. We were sweaty and relieved when we were finally able to peel ourselves off of our seats and out of the vehicle.

The main reason for stopping at Ziguinchor was to get a visa for the neighbouring country, Guinea-Bissau. We had been reliably informed you could get one within a couple of hours on the same day you applied for it. We used a Lonely Planet guide to navigate our way to the street where the embassy was (I prefer not to walk around with my phone out using Google Maps). However, when we arrived at the location listed in the guidebook and there was no embassy in sight, we fairly quickly realised we were in the wrong place. So much for a quick visa.

After speaking to a very friendly and help-ful lady in the French consulate on the same street, we worked out that in reality it was a further 10-minute walk away. By the time we arrived at the embassy we were worried we might have missed the opening hours as it was coming up to 12 and the French consulate closed then. Thankfully it was open and after waiting just 10 minutes we were served. We paid the 20000 CFA (about £40) and were issued visas on the spot. I have never been issued a visa so quickly, especially not in Africa, so to celebrate we went for lunch at a slightly pricey expat restaurant. It had the added benefit of Wi-Fi (something we had been without for a day and a half) and cold beers.

Buoyed by our success, we then made a mistake when deciding on our onward travel. At the transport station we went for the cheapest option, which meant a large minibus, instead of a more expensive but definitely quicker Sept-Place. The bus took ages to sell every seat and once all the spaces had been filled the luggage then had to be loaded onto the roof, which was a drawn-out process and turned the bus into a tottering tower, looking like an accident waiting to happen.

After the last bag had been tied down, we set off, but stopped so frequently it was absurd and very frustrating. We had no understanding of Portuguese (the language spoke in Guinea-Bissau), so we could not understand why the stops kept occurring; there just seemed to be a constant stream of arguing between the driver and everyone else on board, with no form of a compromise or resolution.

After dozens of pointless stops, we hit the border, which actually turned out to be straight forward, but again we had to wait ages for the bus and all the luggage to be checked before we could climb back on board. We waited at the side of the road and ate some fresh watermelon to pass the time.

The remainder of the 120 km route from the border to Bissau took over five hours and was equally as slow as the first section. It took so long, partly due to the overloading of the bus and poor roads, but mainly due to the stops which if any-thing had become more frequent after the border. We had expected to arrive in Bissau around seven in the evening, but it was after ten by the time we had our luggage off the bus. We had shawarma for dinner and a few beers to round off a stressful, but typical day on the road in Africa. TIA[7].

Following an okay night's sleep, we headed straight to the Guinean embassy, just before its

---

[7] TIA (This Is Africa) is a phrased used by Africans and non-Africans to show frustration or endearment towards the continent. It is an encouragement to chill out and relax because "these things happen".

scheduled opening as we hoped to beat any potential queues. Surprisingly there was nobody else waiting and when it hit opening hour we were able to speak to one of the staff straight away. He told us we required copies of our passports, Guinea-Bissau visa page and also our yellow fever certificates. In addition, we were told we needed trousers to be seen in the consulate. However, he then delivered the final blow when he said that we would not be able to apply for the visa until the afternoon and even if we were successful, we would only be able to collect our passports and visas in two days' time.

We searched around the surrounding streets and asked numerous people, in both English and terrible French (not that either language is spoken in Guinea-Bissau), where a copier shop might be found. Thankfully, a local man spoke English and directed us to a shop, two blocks away.

The shop was a mess of electrical goods, piled high on both sides. The contents were in no form of order and the old wooden shelves at the rear of the room looked like the workshop of a mad scientist. Underneath a pile of dusty books and paper was a 90's photocopier which, after being turned on, slowly whirred into life, like a dog waking up on a cold morning. After showing the man in the shop (presumably not the owner) how to operate the machine, we duly got the right amount of copies of all the required documents.

Back in our room at the hostel we did some planning for the next two legs of our trip, through the jungle to Guinea and then onto Sierra Leone. We soon realised that with only three days remaining (there was no "quick processing fee" for the visas) and the 24 hours needed for a Sierra Leone visa we would not be able to get to Freetown (Sierra Leone) in time for our flight, which was scheduled for Christmas Eve and we were therefore going to miss it.

We had three options; our first option was to spend Christmas in West Africa, which was tempting as Sierra Leone has some of the most pristine white sand beaches in the world and a beer in the sun would not have been a bad way to spend Christ's birthday. The second option was to attempt to find another way to get to Sierra Leone to make the flight and our last option was to find an alternative way home.

There was no quick way of getting to Conakry, the capital of Guinea. There was either a long road route which typically took two days, or a 12-hour mad dash through the jungle on the back of a motorbike; the latter had already been our favoured option, so we had no way of cutting down the time. We could have tried riding to the border and attempting to bribe the guards, but it would have meant doing the same thing when we exited the country. This would have been a huge risk as it had a low chance of success and could have cost us hundreds of dollars. The practise of bribing was also not something I wanted to encourage or endorse.

Flying over Guinea direct to Sierra Leone was another possibility, but the prohibitive cost of tickets put us off; even when we tried changing the dates around by a day or two, it was still hundreds of pounds each. Discarding this as a viable option we then checked our tickets to see if they could be changed or refunded; we only ever thought there was an outside chance but worth trying. Our excellent planning back in England had led us to find the cheapest possible flights to the African continent, which of course meant our tickets were non-refundable, non-transferable and there were no exceptions. The airline's web-site made that absolutely clear.

The only other option available to us was to see what new flights we could book to get us back to the UK in time for Christmas. We cast our net far and wide in the hopes of finding the cheapest deal possible. We looked at flights from Dakar (a regional airline hub), Conakry, Bamako in Mali, as well as from Bissau. The internet in the hostel had been a constant pain, testing our patience as searches would buffer slowly then drop out before fully loading. With our stress levels high and our patience just about at breaking point, I messaged one of my best friends, Harri, to assist us. She did an excellent job, finding dozens of options to choose from.

Flights from Dakar were quite a lot cheaper than flying from Bissau, however the hassle of two extra days traveling just to get back there and the cost of transport (as well as the additional stress) put us off the idea and we decided it was not worth it. So, in the end, Harri booked the two of us onto a flight from Bissau to Casablanca, where we then hoped to be able to get our connecting flight back to the UK the following day.

After relieving our bank accounts of a sizeable sum, we went for some tomato rice and fish (traditional local food which meant it was cheap) and then explored the city of Bissau. It was actually a refreshing feeling knowing that for once we were not time constrained and did not have to rush off to the nearest transport hub any time that day. It turned out to be the first and only time during the trip that we actually stayed in the same place for more than one night.

Believe it or not, there is actually not that much to do in Bissau. We walked to the port, which was in the old colonial district of the city. In its heyday it would undoubtedly have been very impressive, now however, it was rundown, dilapidated and you needed a 4x4 to traverse most of the roads. None of the streets were paved and a lot had huge craters in them, meaning traffic just disregarded rules of the road and swerved all over the place. Next we explored one of the local markets, which was down some very small alleys leading right into the heart of a huge warren.

After being overwhelmed by the smells of spices, fresh fish, hanging meat, leather goods and piles of fruit, we were ready to see the light of day again. However, it was not as simple as just walking out, as each turn took us into another alley; the whole place was a maze. We eventually emerged back onto a main road and treated ourselves to an Arabic tea (a small glass of black tea with an unhealthy amount of sugar). We were then able to enjoy spending the rest of the day relaxing and having a day off from travelling.

Despite only having spent one day in the capital, we had exhausted Bissau of all its entertainment value. We cast our net further afield and caught a minibus and then a taxi to a small town called Qinhamel, about 35km outside the city. The town itself was little more than a tarred street running through a collection of buildings, however, on the left-hand side of the road there was a narrow, dirt track running slightly downhill towards the river. It was here that we hoped to find a beach.

It had been recommended by both our hostel owner and the guidebook, so we thought it must be half decent. The track down was very odd and appeared to be out of place with the surrounding area. It was lined with large trees all the way down to the river. They were probably planted in days gone by, when the Portuguese still ran the country. The trees remained a mystery. We could not work out why they had been planted, as the road did not lead to a large house or any other grand structure, but instead just petered out at the water's edge.

The place we found ourselves at was unrecognisable as a beach to any European. Not in a million years would you find its picture in a holiday magazine or tour company brochure. It was nothing more than a muddy bank of the river. We struggled to see why it had been so highly recommended.

The beach was actually so unpleasant I was put off from even wanting to lay my towel on it.

There was no sand or pebbles, just mud. The alternative was small rocks covered in broken glass; we opted for the latter and laid out some rugs and our towels to add some comfort. The water was also a disappointment and far too shallow to swim in, because it was low tide and even by the time we left, a couple of hours later, it would not have reached your waist had you gone out into the deepest section.

The third un-beach like feature we noticed was that there was absolutely nobody else in sight, although we had been told it was very popular with the locals; maybe it was the fact that we visited on a Thursday. However, the lack of people did mean we could sunbathe without being constantly stared at for being so white. We enjoyed a couple of hours trying to coax some colour into our skin, to have at least some proof that we had been travelling in Africa.

Later in the day, just as we were heading out for dinner, another backpacker turned up, a Ukrainian called Orest. He joined us for shawarma and a couple of beers, before we had to pack and head to the airport to fly to Morocco first thing the following morning.

We were at the airport by 01:00. Our flight left from Bissau for Casablanca at 04:30, so we could check in almost immediately and sailed through security. We both attempted to nap in the departure lounge, but it was not until we were aboard the plane that we could properly get comfortable and sleep.

Once we had landed in Casablanca, we took a train to the centre of the city and found a cute little cafe for a late breakfast. I had a Moroccan breakfast, which consisted of orange juice, bread and a tagine of egg and meat, which was amazing, as well as mint tea, which was a pleasant change from the weak coffee we had predominantly been drinking.

Casablanca is a much larger city than many capitals in Africa; for a start it has high rise buildings, which we had not seen since Dakar. Secondly it takes ages to walk anywhere, so we decided to get a taxi to our hostel from the other side of the city. Unfortunately, our driver liked picking up other people on the way and dropping them off 'en route', which meant a 10/15-minute journey turned into an hour. We complained but our protests were ignored.

The hour turned into even longer as it became apparent that the driver had no idea where we wanted to go. After asking for directions three times he still struggled to comprehend where we needed to go, so we alighted near to the hostel and walked the remainder of the way with the aid of Google Maps. It was most certainly quicker and by that point we had both had enough of the terrible tunes which had been playing constantly. After this we decided to walk everywhere.

Our accommodation was an up-market backpacker hostel, with social areas and decent enough rooms, as well as good Wi-Fi, which made a pleasant change to Guinea-Bissau and the majority of the rest of the West African coast. Despite the tortuous journey to reach the hostel, it was not long before we headed back towards the city centre and the coast. The main (and arguably only) sight to see in the city is the Hassan II Mosque, which is the 13th largest mosque in the world and has the world's tallest minaret. I will admit that it was pretty impressive. The inside is meant to be beautiful, but unfortunately we were unable to have a look, as it was a Friday and prayers were in full swing. The only other sights of note in Casablanca were the artisan shops dotted around, which were vaguely interesting, but nothing to the sheer scale, quantity or variety that Marrakech offers; we gave them a cursory glance over before going to find some food.

For our last dinner of the trip we purposely chose food to use up our collective remaining money. We opted for pizzas, which were cheap and filling, before getting the last train of the day to the airport, where we had a short wait. We yet again attempted to sleep (unsuccessfully) before we boarded and flew back to the UK, landing on Christmas Eve morning to much relief from the family.

THREE BECOMES ONE

On my return from a mountaineering trip in the Himalayas I briefly returned to the UK to leave my cold weather clothing and expedition kit at home and also because crazily it was cheaper to fly back to the UK and then to Vietnam, than it was to fly from Nepal to Vietnam direct. This time I was embarking on a backpacking trip with two of my friends, Rob and George, who I had just spent the last seven years with at school. We had an epic four-month, unplanned adventure in South East Asia lined up, a classic Gap Year trip, but one which would contribute to my travel passion.

We flew into Hanoi, in northern Vietnam, to begin our trip. After a couple of days sojourn in Ha Long Bay we made our way south along the coast, stopping at every town along the way, even if there was nothing 'touristy' to do there. We had a great laugh and experienced some awesome things together; including some epic motorcycle rides, SCUBA diving and many visits to temples; but it was always destined to fail. We ultimately wanted to do and see different things on this trip; theirs involved substantially more alcohol and sleep than mine[8].

We had previously discussed our different opinions on how to travel and until this point we had democratically decided what to do on any particular day by having a vote; nine times out of 10 I would be in the minority. I would then have two options: go along with their plan or spend the day by myself. The first two weeks of our trip I went with the pack mentality, but I started to become more and more independent of the other two.

After about three weeks on the road together I became frustrated with my friends. Typically, we would explore a new town, or something in the local vicinity, during the day, eat dinner out and then invariably end up in a bar. My issue with this was that the following morning I continued to rise at eight, despite how I might feel, but I was unable to coerce the other two into getting up. Usually I sat and read for a while until they felt fresh enough to start another day of exploring. However, by this stage I had

---

[8] Not that I don't like a good drink.

had enough. I had not spent the last two years working at the weekends, and then on a fulltime basis for a couple of months, getting paid the minimum wage of £3.71 an hour (for an under 18) to waste money on drink and my precious time asleep.

We were staying in the beautiful seaside town of Mũi Né, which has a beach lined with palm trees and a small fishing community. We had been there a couple of nights already but had decided we would treat ourselves to a night in a hotel. I checked out of the hostel before the other two, made my way a bit further down the coast and headed for our first hotel. Here I dropped my bags and picked up some oats, fresh fruit and yogurt for breakfast and a Vietnamese coffee. The coffee can be served either hot or as an iced drink; it is a slow drip brewing process which is then mixed with condensed milk. Despite normally opting for an Americano with no milk or sugar, I absolutely loved this slightly sweet concoction.

After a chilled start to the day I made my way back to the hostel and bumped into George and Rob. They had no plans apart from sitting on the beach all day, but I intended to make the most of my time, so I booked myself onto a mini tour. After a couple of hours reading, I headed out with a small group in the back of an old US Army

Jeep. I am not sure if the Jeep was a relic of the war, or an imported modern version, either way the fresh breeze from the open top took away the heat of the day.

We trekked up a nearby river and as the water was between ankle and knee deep we waded up, which in 40-degree heat was a refreshing experience. We followed this by exploring one of the bays littered with fishing boats, old nets and even older looking fishermen mending the nets. Around Mũi Né there are huge sand dunes which we climbed up and tried to sandboard down. Despite our best efforts nobody managed to race down the slope, ending up with a face full of hot sand for our efforts. To finish off the tour we trekked up an impressive red coloured sand dune to watch the sunset. The whole day was spent with an international mix of people, but we all shared the same travel values. It was a reminder of why I had embarked on this trip in the first place.

On my return to the hotel I met the boys and we went off for dinner - our last one together before we would split paths. The meal was an interesting affair; I ordered some of the tastiest tiger prawns I have ever had, freshly caught and cooked on an open fire and George and Rob went for snake - more precisely cobra. The head was cut off in front of us, the blood was poured into a glass (after it was mixed with vodka, they both drank a shot of it) and the heart was cut out. Rob ate the heart whilst it was still beating (apparently in Vietnamese culture it is a show of masculinity). The snake was also cooked on the open fire and once ready the meat itself was really tasty but a challenge to remove from the bones.

The following morning, I yet again woke before the other two and had packed, checked out and gone for breakfast before they were even up. I had booked my ticket to Ho Chi Minh City (I think it is a silly name; the equivalent would be calling London "Winston Churchill" or even worse "Teresa May"). It is locally known as Saigon, the traditional name for the city.

George and Rob, meanwhile, had decided to catch a bus to Vientiane (the capital of Laos). It was by no means just around the corner, as the bus journey would take 50 hours. They planned to meet up with some other guys from school who were travelling in South East Asia at the same time. So this was the parting of our ways. There were no hard feelings and we had even arranged to meet up in Thailand in a few weeks. But for me now it meant going solo and travelling by myself for the next three months.

My journey to Ho Chi Minh City was uneventful. For nearly four hours I allowed Stephen Fry to serenade me as I listened to Harry Potter and the Chamber of Secrets. The rest of the six-hour journey I either read or gazed out of the window. When we arrived, there was the usual crush of taxi drivers and hotel reps, which is a common experience in backpacker-heavy locations. One guy offered me a room for $5. It was good deal and late in the evening and I was hungry, so I accepted and followed him. In my room there were 9 beds; I met five of the other occupants - a Spaniard, who never said a word, and four other English guys from Surrey, who were really friendly and welcomed me into their group. Together we sought out some street food, which was unbelievably tasty.

My first night alone was a great one. It was easy to make conversation with strangers and they in turn were happy for me to tag along. This initial experience continued for the entire duration of my trip. Everywhere I went there were friendly people, who welcomed me into their groups, or other solo travellers. Sometimes my interactions would only go as far as meeting people for a drink, but on occasions I spent a week or more with them, as we got along well and were travelling in the same direction.

Many of those I met on the road I remain in contact with via social media (the perks of travel in the twenty-first century). Since this first foray into solo travel I have ventured on dozens of trips by myself and love it. I would recommend it to anyone, as you discover a lot about yourself and it gives you plenty of time to think. The cliché of 'finding yourself' whilst travelling is pretty spot on when talking of solo travel. There are never conversations about "what are we going to do today?" and you can see and do whatever you want, whenever you fancy it.

There are some potential downsides too, as you often spend extended periods of time by yourself, which can take a while to adjust to. I have discovered, though, that there are always other travellers or locals willing to spend time with you and possibly become travel buddies for a couple of days or weeks. I have definitely realised I have more personal interactions when I travel alone. For me solo travel far outweighs group travel, although there is arguably a sweet-spot when you find one person with whom you can travel stress free - then I think you have found the best of both worlds.

BELTS, BULLET HOLES AND BANDITS

Two and a half years after I had embarked on my previous road trip, I decided once more to put my faith in the hands of the mechanical gods and at the mercy of the Volvo estate. This time my co-pilot would be my friend, now girlfriend, Harri. The same Harri who helped Nick and me search for new plane tickets home from West Africa[9]. This was our first trip together as a couple.

Harri, a seasoned traveller and lover of adventure, jumped at the idea of a road trip around Eastern Europe and Scandinavia. It was another ambitious route, over 4700 miles, (7500 kilometres) driving from the UK to Poland and then

---

[9] Some of you will have noticed that I have done the impossible and climbed out of the friend zone.

north to Finland and back west through Norway, Sweden and Denmark, before returning to our start point. Sleeping bags and roll mats were ditched and a duvet and a mattress topper replaced them. We also devised a genius home-made curtain. String was tied above the windows and over the front seats and then a blanket was stretched out and trapped by the boot when it was shut, with old sheets hung along the sides, over the string. You could argue there was more of a feminine touch this time around.

We started in earnest driving from Kent, in the South East of England, to Bruges with just a stop for the Channel Tunnel crossing. In Bruges we wandered around the windy cobbled streets in the search for waffles; not too hard in the tourist capital of Belgium. I would describe myself as a food connoisseur (at least to the extent that I have eaten a lot of food in many corners of the world, including more than my fair share of waffles) and in my opinion the waffles in Bruges are the best in the world[10].

The next day, after we had survived our first night, (I can confirm that the mattress topper and duvet were far more comfortable than a sleeping bag), we ate up the miles and made our

---

[10] Data not compiled through an official survey.

way across the whole of Northern Germany, making the most of the autobahns. A couple of years previously, I had been based in Gütersloh with the Army, so we made a slight detour enabling me to show Harri the barracks where I had lived. It was great to visit the town and see that nothing had really changed. We even ate lunch at one of my favourite restaurants[11]. In the afternoon, having covered mile upon mile of the finest German motorway, we finally hit Poland and its beautiful countryside; although I would struggle to say the same for its uneven roads.

That night we stayed near Auschwitz, although it was a challenge to reach. Harri was using Google Maps to direct us and would occasionally tell me to take the next left, just as I was driving past it at 40 mph and then to compensate, she would direct me down the turning before the one we wanted. After a number of U-turns, we eventually made it and found a quiet area to park and sleep.

We had a sombre visit to Auschwitz the next morning and spent a couple of hours wandering around the camp, pretty much in silence, before enjoying a cultured trip to Warsaw in the afternoon. Along the route north out of Poland we stopped in the middle of a forest,

---

[11] It also doubles up as an excellent bar in the evening.

where the road ran straight as an arrow through tall pine trees for a number of kilometres. There were no other vehicles on the road, just us. We pulled over and spent time taking photos in the middle of the road; these are now some of my favourite photos.

After four days and hundreds of miles of driving, we crossed over into Lithuania. We had booked a room in a hotel as a treat after sleeping in the car for three nights. Thanks to charges being dropped on mobile roaming, Harri was able to book whilst I was driving. But as fate would have it, we were not destined to stay in the car that night anyway. Not far out of Vilnius, the capital of Lithuania, the car began having problems (most important of which was the AC and radio stopped working). Trying to negotiate tight turns in Vilnius Old Town without power steering in a long wheelbase, one and a half tonne car was not easy. I had to do a three-point turn to get the Volvo off the road and into the hotel car park.

Despite the poorly car parked outside, we had a great evening of pizza and wine. I also tried a local delicacy of pig's ear - I would not recommend it - and then took the ailing car to a Volvo garage on the edge of the city the following morning. The car almost did not make it, barely juddering onto the forecourt. The guy who inspected it gave us the bad news that one of the motors had broken (the reason the electrics stopped) and this had then put strain on the alternator belt and had broken another motor. Despite not being a car mechanic (you might have guessed by my description of what was wrong), I knew that the repairs were not going to be cheap.

We were quoted the equivalent of £650 and told to come back the following afternoon. As this was rather a painful amount, which we had not budgeted for, we moved out of our hotel and into the cheapest hostel we could find. We regretted the eight-man room later, when what can only be described as the worst snoring I have ever heard erupted out of the man in the bunk next to me. Neither of us could stop laughing and we struggled to understand how some people slept through it. However, the delay did give us an extra two days to explore Vilnius, see all its sights and eat in some amazing local restaurants.

The following afternoon we returned to the garage, picked up the car (now with working AC, radio and power steering) and hit the road once again. Our trip was back on track; Harri was back to feeding in new CDs and researching our next stop and I was behind the wheel again. We were making good progress and were driving north to Latvia through a string of small towns when there was a bang and I lost all power to the car. I managed to coast the Volvo off the road and into a layby and then assessed the situation. Somehow, despite having a brand-new belt fitted in Vilnius, it had snapped.

Once again, I was standing at the side of the road in a foreign country with a broken-down car. We were transported to a garage that had a lock up car park and informed, via the Lithuanian branch of AA, that we had a hotel booked and the car would be towed to a garage the next morning for an assessment.

However, what the very helpful lady at the AA did not realise, was that the lock up car park was in fact full of car wrecks, including one which had a dozen bullet holes strewn across the windscreen and, if you peered in and looked closely, brown stains on the seats. We found it quite funny, but the video we sent to Harri's safety-conscious mum received a less than welcome reception.

Once we had safely made it out of the (car) graveyard and to our hotel, we lightened the mood in the best way we knew; cheap wine and even cheaper pizza, consumed whilst watching one of Netflix's offerings. A good end to another frustrating day on the road.

The good news was that the car was fixed and ready to roll early the following afternoon. One of the motors had not been affixed properly and had managed to rattle loose, which led to the belt snapping[12]. Our spirits were high as we drove on further north, crossed over the border into Latvia and made it to Riga; another beautiful capital city, full of culture and great food (and wine)[13]. We enjoyed exploring the old streets, marvelling at the architecture and just sitting outside in the sun, soaking up the atmosphere.

From Riga, we continued north on a beautiful road which hugged the coastline all the way up across the border and onto Parnu in Estonia. It would have been rude not to stop at one of the beaches en route. In the early evening we set off for a swim, then walked along to the end of the beach, where there was a rock pier which we clambered over to the end, enjoying an uninterrupted view out to sea.

We continued driving along the coast into Estonia and when the sun started to drop towards the horizon we pulled over at another beach. This one had a boardwalk, which took us through a

---

[12] The Volvo garage admitted fault and refunded the cost of the second garage's fees. Just a shame they could not refund time.

[13] Did I mention we like wine?

field of reeds, before reaching a secluded beach which was virtually empty. We had brought a bottle of Baileys from England with us, which although a traditional Christmas drink to most people, went down very well on a sandy beach in the middle of summer in southern Estonia, whilst watching the setting sun. It proved a wonderful contrast to our previous evening in the car graveyard.

We slept nearby in a layby, next to a field dotted with bales of hay. In the morning, we continued up the coast and then inland towards the capital, Tallinn. Once there, we explored and visited each tourist attraction in turn, including a Medieval themed restaurant which Lonely Planet described as having "costumed wenches" as waitresses. I found Tallinn a huge surprise, with the lovely open market square and the winding, colourful streets. It is safe to say that it lived up to our expectations

Tallinn is on the coast and no day by the sea would be complete without watching the sunset on a beach. Another bottle of wine was found and a couple of hours were spent gazing out to sea, chatting about everything and nothing before wandering back along the beach to the car.

Our original plan had been to cross over to Helsinki and drive up and around the Gulf of

Bothnia (the expanse of water that separates Finland from Sweden), driving through some of the most beautiful scenery in the world. However, thanks to our old car and dodgy mechanics, we had lost a couple of days of driving. After exploring numerous options to retrieve time (and over 1000 miles of driving), we settled on heading up to Helsinki and then across to a port on the west coast called Turku, where we could catch a ferry the following morning to Stockholm.

After traditional and hearty meals of reindeer, moose and all kinds of seafood, we left Finland and made the 11-hour crossing to Sweden. The sea, just outside of Turku, was littered with small islands; some with just a single, tiny log cabin, others with whole villages and still others completely empty. The entire archipelago was one of the most beautiful natural formations I have ever seen. When we neared Stockholm (after a nap in the Volvo on the car deck and having played dozens of card games), there were again hundreds of small islets, beautiful and remote, portraying a lifestyle far away from the distractions of the 21st Century. We both said we would love to sail around them one day and I really hope we do.

In Stockholm we were treated to a night out of the Volvo staying with a couple of Harri's friends and chatting late into the evening, not realising it was midnight, as it was still light outside, due to being so far north. The following morning, we said our goodbyes and set off in search of a supermarket to stock up with road supplies. We found a huge shop called WiLLY:S; with our youthful senses of humour, we found it so funny we just had to go in.

Sweden is famous for its vast number of lakes and with the sun shining on the water we could not resist plunging into at least one of them. One of the things I love about road tripping is the freedom it gives you to explore beyond the cities, allowing you to experience so much more of the country. You also have the freedom to spontaneously stop whenever you wish.

We drove down a track to a campsite, grabbed our towels and hiked around the edge of the lake. We had passed nobody and there were only a couple of people on the lake sailing, a long way off, so we stripped off and jumped in. Never before has water felt so refreshing. We had just clambered out and were drying off when a family walked around the headland, along the path above us; perfect timing. We had a good laugh about it on the way back to the car and then continued to drive west across the country towards Norway.

That night we pulled off the main road, down a single width track into the forest. We drove until we were well embedded in the wood, the noise of the road had disappeared and there was just the sound of nature. We slept like babies.

Along with driving around the Gulf of Bothnia, we also had to miss out driving along the beautiful Norwegian Coastal Road and visiting some of the Fjords. We decided we did not want to rush either, so missed them both out and vowed to return at some point in the future. Instead we headed to Oslo and visited the impressive architectural structure of the Oslo Opera House and the Akershus Slott (Oslo's fortress). We had been excited to explore one of the most expensive cities in the world; however, we quickly decided that everything was far too pricey for our meagre budget and returned to the car.

Leaving Oslo and its exorbitant prices behind us, we drove into the evening. Although we had missed out on seeing the fjords, we still wanted to experience a little bit of coastal Norway, so we headed off the motorway near Rygge and down to the coast. Once again we had some wine whilst watching the sunset over the water (have you noticed a theme yet). There is something special about a large body of water and the setting sun; a magical feeling which trapped us in the moment. The amazing experience was continued at the campsite with people on holiday having campfires and BBQs in the late evening sun.

We continued our journey the next day, back into Sweden and on to Denmark. We drove over the Øresund, a huge bridge which turns into a tunnel, connecting the two countries. We had no idea quite how long it was until we crossed over; perhaps the expensive toll charge should have given us a clue.

We had both visited Denmark before, but we were very generously hosted by some family friends, Richard and Mette and their children, staying in their spare room. Richard grew up with my parents and then fell in love with Denmark and its inhabitants. Despite Denmark being an awesome country (my words not his) and the fact it is now his home he does pine for "England's green and pleasant land." We explored the city, admired the cool coffee shops and Scandi furniture (like any good tourist would) and then were made to feel at home and fed well by Richard and Mette.

Forever onwards, we drove through The Netherlands stopping in Amsterdam. By this point we had mastered the art of parking in big cities, so found a carpark on the outskirts and caught the famous tram into the centre. When we arrived we wandered around the canals and ate brunch with some friends from our home town, who were coincidently there for the weekend, before continuing onto Bruges once more for no other reason than to get another waffle (I did say they were good).

We drove into France and arrived in Calais by early evening. We parked in free parking behind some residential buildings and searched for some dinner. Calais struck me as very like a British seaside resort - slightly worn out, past its heyday, but still with a little character and charm. We found a cute restaurant, where we enjoyed one of the tastiest meals of the trip; we both had a kilogram of fresh mussels and paid €11 each – an absolute bargain.

Back at the car we set up our makeshift curtains and settled down to sleep for our last night on the road. A couple of hours later we were woken by shouting nearby. We both lay awake wondering what was happening. We peeked out of the back of the car, through a gap in the blanket and saw a full-blown argument between two opposing groups of people[14]. Hoping that they,

---

[14] Definitely looked like two gangs to me.

like a storm, would eventually tire and be quiet, we tried to get some sleep. However, the noise increased and the argument became more violent, with pushing and screaming. We could not understand the French, so we were unable to work out what the argument was about, but it certainly was not a peaceful conversation. It also looked as if at least one of the men was holding a pistol, although in the dim light, 20 metres away it was hard to tell. I was not intending to get any closer to check it out.

After some time, one of the group noticed our car, decided to investigate and came walking towards it. Harri, visibly scared, asked if the doors were locked. I reassured her and promised I had locked them all before we had gone to sleep.

We quickly laid back down, shut our eyes and pretended to be asleep. The individual had a torch and shone it into the car, through the small gaps we had around the hung sheets. As the light flickered across our faces we tried not to move, as it would give up the game that we were not in fact asleep.

All the while we were playing sleeping lions, I was wondering if I had indeed locked the doors. When I told Harri that I had locked them, I was about ninety-nine percent sure that I had, but now my certainty had dropped to 95 percent, a figure which was reducing by the minute! I played out different scenarios in my head, where the torch wielding man tried to open the door. What would I do and more importantly, what could I do if he did? By the time the man had finished inspecting the inside of the car, concluding that we were asleep and walked off, I estimated that my confidence that I had locked the doors was down to about 20 percent.

Thankfully about half an hour after this incident the whole group dispersed; nobody had been shot and we were able to breath freely again, without thinking our lives were in danger. We quickly pulled the sheets down; I jumped into the driver's seat and with Harri still under the duvet in the boot, we drove to another car park, much better lit, within sight of the main road. We were more conspicuous, but safe; there were even a number of CCTV cameras to keep an eye on us.

Morning came far too early, especially after such a sleepless night, but we had an early crossing back to England away from the gangs of Calais. It was important that we made the crossing, because that same day I was also moving from one Army barracks to another, due to starting a different job the following day. There is nothing quite like a relaxing holiday.

TRAVELLING SOLO

FLIGHT FROM HELL

Having travelled all around the world to dozens of countries, many of which I have visited by plane, it was inevitable that out of the couple of hundred flights I have taken that there was going to be at least one which was a disaster.

This fateful trip started in chilly Northern Germany, at Gütersloh train station, where I was based with the Army at the time. It was a fairly non-descript Saturday in the mid-afternoon when I set off; the journey would end in a much warmer Belize, albeit a couple of days later than I had originally expected.

I initially boarded a train bound for Frankfurt; three changes, a 20-minute delay and five hours of reading later I arrived at Frankfurt Airport. This left me with plenty of time to check in for my evening flight. The first airborne leg of my journey was to Manchester, just a short hop back to the Land of Hope and Glory.

Despite not being my final destination, it was nice to be 'home', even briefly. We landed late at night and then I had an excruciatingly long 11-hour layover before my next flight left the following morning at 09:30. When I originally booked my flight, (the cheapest one available), this layover featured low on my list of concerns, but perhaps this was an error on my part

Being very money conscious and not wanting to pay for a night at one of the nearby, overpriced, airport hotels, I spent a rather uncomfortable night lying on the airport floor. I resorted to using my towel as a mattress and my extremely thin, sleeping bag liner as a cover - not something I would recommend. Even if you include my Army training at Sandhurst and the exercises I have been on since, that night was still one of the least comfortable, chilliest and sleep deprived I have ever spent[15].

As I could not fall asleep, I got up just before five, packed up my 'bed' and found the only café open that early in the morning and bought a croissant for breakfast and a black coffee, in an attempt to stave off tiredness. I then moved from the Arrivals Lounge into Departures to wait and for a change of scenery. At 06:30 I was

---

[15] Note to self: Pay for a hotel next time.

eventually allowed to check in, but more hanging around awaited me. Once I had made a speedy passage through security, (there was virtually nobody else at the airport that early in the morning), I was very relieved when I finally heard the announcement to start boarding the Thomas Cook flight to Cancun. My body was extremely ready for the flight to get underway so I could fall asleep.

The journey itself was one of the longest I have ever been on and I was especially thankful that I could finally rest my head and catch up on some much-needed rest. All was going well until I was woken up for some food, then woken again not long after for the drinks trolley and then again for some more food a couple of hours later. In the end I just gave up and watched some films.

Half an hour before we were due to land the captain came on the intercom to announce that the radar was broken at Cancun Airport. This meant we could not land until it was fixed (just what everyone wanted to hear). We joined a holding pattern, but two hours and four loops later we were informed that we were running out of fuel, (more good news), and so we would have to land at Cozumel[16] as the radar was still not functioning.

As it transpired, we were not the only flight to land at Cozumel; in fact, we were fifth in line to fill up and a number of other planes joined us shortly afterwards. Not long after we had landed and whilst still in the queue for fuel, a large storm blew up and appeared to set in for the evening. This meant that no refuelling could happen whilst there was lightning.

During this extended wait on the runway the engines had to be turned off, to ensure we still had enough fuel to taxi to the fuelling pump. Then to make matters even worse, and to add insult to considerable injury, the emergency batteries were drained of electricity. This in turn meant the main lights cut out and the air-conditioning stopped operating, much to everyone's delight.

The lack of working air-con turned the cabin into a sauna. It was sweltering and very humid. Everyone on board was wafting themselves with in-flight magazines or whatever they had to hand; babies and children were crying and several people, mainly middle-aged, overweight

---

[16] An island just south of Cancun, popular with cruise ships.

men (probably all British) took off their shirts. The Cabin Crew were certainly in an unenviable position; I have never felt so sorry for a group of people.

This stressful situation continued for well over an hour. During this time all the water on board the plane had been drunk and I was contemplating joining in with the half-dozen babies who were screaming, (not really, but it was a frustrating situation to find yourself in). As if the situation could not have disintegrated any further, concurrently to all the other problems we were experiencing, our two pilots ran out of flying hours, so we had to wait for another crew to be flown out from Cancun (now open) to come and replace them.

At long last, with tempers worn very thin, (a few people's had definitely worn through), the plane was refuelled, a fresh crew was at the helm and we were able to set off. We landed in Cancun just before midnight, almost eight hours late. For most of my fellow passengers they had just experienced a hugely uncomfortable flight and lost an afternoon of a package holiday; but for me it meant I had also missed a connecting flight to Belize, from where I had been intending to start my adventures.

However, my travel woes were not yet over; unfortunately they were not even close to being over. I spent nearly two stressful hours at the airport, trying to establish what was going to happen with me and when I would be able to fly to Belize to start my journey through Central America. Eventually I managed to pin someone down who would both listen to me and also had the powers to do something about my situation. Just after one in the morning I was informed that I would not be flying any time soon. There was nothing else to be done, other than to go to a hotel, where I was assured I would be contacted as soon as they had any information on my onward flight. Back in the UK the Thomas Cook offices were shut, so apparently "nothing could be done now". It was not the start of the trip I had hoped for.

On the positive side, the hotel was rather plush, certainly compared to the hostels and cheap hotels I usually stay in. It was an all-inclusive, five-star resort, where other customers were probably paying over £150 a night. I was very appreciative of this but I would still rather have been sleeping in a bamboo hut on a beach in Belize, as I had originally planned.

When I woke in the morning at about 09:00 I was slightly worried that I had not heard anything regarding my flight, so I went and used the telephone behind the lobby desk to ring 'my man', Cori. Five phone calls and two hours later he told me that he had booked me onto the 14:00 flight to Belize City. Better late than never I thought. However, to my dismay, my jubilation was short lived as less than 10 minutes later one of the bell boys came to find me in my room to say that Cori was on the phone again. When I got back to reception and spoke to him, he told me that he had made a mistake and the flight was actually 14:00 tomorrow, not today.

Disappointed, but realising there was nothing I could do other than cross a day of SCUBA diving in Belize's Blue Hole off my list, I went to the bar. On the plus side, I had another night in the all-inclusive hotel; not the way I typically like to spend my holiday, or the way I had planned to spend my time in Central America, but I enjoyed relaxing nonetheless.

The following day, after a buffet breakfast, I received a phone call telling me my transport to the airport had arrived. This time I hoped the flight was scheduled for the correct day. I did not want to lose any more days from my trip. The driver appeared surprised with my backpacking attire: old walking shoes, faded t-shirt and rucksack with flag patches sewn on; his expression confirmed that I did not fit the usual client appearance.

Nevertheless, we set off and he drove me to a small, random building near the international airport, stopped and told me to get out. Slightly confused I enquired as to why we had stopped. Apparently, it was where Tropic Air (my airline) flew from. Still not fully believing him I got out and went inside the building. Sure enough inside there were a couple of check in desks and a 30-seat departure lounge (I had plenty of time to count). With my flight not leaving for another two and a half hours I had ample time to do some reading - not that there were any other options.

When we finally made our way out onto the apron and onto the plane, a small 15-seater, I struggled to see how there was not a spare seat on the flight yesterday, as only eight passengers were assigned seats on my flight. You could not stand up inside the plane and being the youngest, and almost certainly the most agile, I made my way to the front, sitting directly behind the pilot and his very attractive co-pilot. Aviators appeared to be an obligatory accessory.

It was quite surreal and very amusing to look out of the front of the plane, through the cockpit, whilst we were lined up on the runway. We were in a queue behind commercial jumbo jets, all of which looked far more suitable to be conducting an international flight than we did. If planes were compared to birds, they were the equivalent to eagles and we were flying in a sparrow.

The two-hour flight was probably the most enjoyable part of my journey so far; we flew low and had views out to both sides and ahead. Through the cockpit, I was able to watch the changing terrain unfold around us as we made our way further south.

After we landed I sailed through passport control and customs as I had no hold baggage and was out the other side in no time. Once outside I quickly walked two miles in the sun to the main highway and hopped onto a local 'chicken' bus. The journey to Belize City via bus cost just two Belize dollars (about £0.70) compared to the 50 Belize dollars a taxi would have cost. The buses are colloquially named Chicken Buses due to their usual occupants transporting all manner of baggage, including chickens and other livestock, with them on their journeys.

Despite now being in Belize, my travel problems continued, but this time it was my fault, at least partially so. Having been delayed two days in Mexico I had had to cut my plans in Belize short, (basically I did not have time to go scuba diving). After a day of exploring Belize City I decided to get a mid-morning bus the following day (the earliest possible opportunity) to head to Tikal, a collection of Mayan temples, in Guatemala. Unfortunately for me no public transport from Belize goes there directly. The only option is to ask the driver to stop at a junction where you can disembark from the buses headed to Flores and make your own way along the last stretch of the journey by catching a microbus or a taxi on towards Tikal. This is what I had planned to do.

The border crossing was pretty straight forward, however, the problems started when I reached the junction. I had read online that there were normally lots of buses going to Flores, which would disgorge passengers wishing to go directly to the temples, meaning that there would be plenty of people with whom to share a taxi fare. However, when my bus arrived, I was the only one who wanted to go to Tikal that evening and there were no more buses expected that day.

Knowing that I had no other options, I was quoted 70 dollars by a taxi driver for the journey to the temples, as I would be the sole occupant. After much talking and bartering, including being driven down the road to a dubious looking tourist office and being offered a full tour of Guatemala (for a couple of thousand dollars) I eventually expressed my displeasure at the price and said I would not be using the driver's services. I left his office and walked back to the junction with the genius plan of just walking to Flores to save money. That was until I saw a sign and realised it was 28 km away and not the couple of kilometres down the road that I believed it to be. I realised that unless some traffic drove past me I was in for a very long walk.

To my relief, a microbus heading in that direction drove past me, just beyond the junction. With slight desperation I chased after it and managed to flag it down. It was extremely cramped in the back, once I had clambered aboard, but it was still 100 times better than walking for six hours. I was dropped on the outskirts of Flores, in a slightly run-down area of the town and caught a tuk tuk to the centre of the old district, where all the hotels were to be found and where I hoped to find somewhere to stay.

At last I was in the right place, albeit over an hour later than the bus would have taken and about seven dollars lighter than I would have been had I just stayed on board in the first place. I was just walking along a street when I spotted an older couple from my bus, who I had chatted to at the border. At the same time, they also recognised me and smiled, so I walked over and chatted about my escapades, which they both found very funny, making me feel rather better, although slightly embarrassed by my ordeal.

I found a hostel and booked tickets for both Tikal and a trip to Antigua (a beautiful colonial town further south), which was two and a half times cheaper than the price 'Mr Taxi Man' had offered me. At least that was one correct decision I had made that evening.

I woke at 04:30 the following morning in order to drive 63km to Tikal and get there in time for the sunrise. Once we were there I parted from the rest of the group and went to explore; they had paid for a tour guide, whereas I always prefer to explore by myself. In a tour group you have to travel at the pace of the slowest person, you only get to stop when the guide tells you to and you only see what the guide wants to show you; to me it feels a bit like being in a straightjacket.

It turned out to be a great decision. I immediately headed to the main plaza where two of the largest and most famous temples are situated (imaginatively named Temples I and II). After exploring a while, I hiked further into the jungle past Temple III which is yet to be excavated. To me, the temple, half hidden by jungle and a mound of earth, gave me the impression of what the first explorers of this site might have experienced and seen back in the Nineteenth Century. My exploration took me deeper into the forest and onto Temple IV, which is the tallest temple and whose highest point can be accessed via a flight of long wooden stairs.

Whilst sitting on Temple IV (63m high) you could see right across the roof of the jungle canopy, which stretched out in every direction, as far as the eye could see. Poking through the trees were the tops of Temples I, II, III and V, impressive structures built to honour long dead kings of a long extinct society.

The tranquillity was amazing, with only the tropical birds making any sound. It was occasionally broken by howler monkeys who made an absolute racket, sounding like dinosaur roars and giving me the feeling of being in another world. It was a truly special place where one could spend hours just sitting and enjoying the views in peace.

One of the favourite places I have ever visited thanks to the adventure getting there, the sense of discovery when exploring the area and the peacefulness atop the temple. It just had a certain *je ne sais quoi* about it that is hard to describe; it was certainly well worth the huge effort it had taken to get there over the preceding few days.

A STEPPE TOO FAR

I failed miserably to get a visa for Uzbekistan in the UK before I departed for Central Asia. I had even taken a day off work and trekked all the way down to the embassy in Kensington and waited in a long queue in their basement office, only to be told I could come and collect my passport in a week's time, two days after my flight to Central Asia departed. This clearly was not an option, so I asked for all my forms, photos, cheque and passport back and sulkily walked away from the counter, realising that my poor admin may have ruined my three-week trip.

This terrible planning in England meant that after a couple of days exploring the north of Kazakhstan, I made my way to Almaty (in the south) and my primary goal was to obtain a visa. I had read that you should arrive at the embassy early, as there would be a sheet where you write your name down and you are served in the order of arrival. Being British, I liked this idea of a formal queue, but I liked the sound of being at the front of it even more.

I set my alarm to wake me at 06:30 and I was at the embassy by 07:15, a full 45 minutes before opening time. However, this still put me 12th on the list; I could not believe that there were 11 other people who wanted a visa more than me. I also did not know if 12th was good or bad; I had no concept of how many people were seen in a day. I did, however, start to feel that 12th was a good place in the queue as more and more people turned up, plenty of them westerners.

The Uzbek embassy was meant to open at 08:00, but there was not even as much as a curtain moving inside. Another hour went by and still nothing. However much I loved the idea of sitting on a kerb all day, I actually had other things I would rather be doing. Thankfully, just after nine, a hatch opened and started serving people. Not being able to speak the language, it took a while to realise that it was not the visa office, but just a man answering enquiries (I think). The consulate part (where they issue visas) did not open until 10:20, well over two hours later than it said on their brass plaque on the wall outside.

A bonus though was that, by this point, I had edged my way up the rankings and was now fifth in the queue. However, to my dismay when I arrived at one of the worn, wooden desks and spoke to a surly member of staff, I was told I had insufficient paperwork to apply for a visa, despite having everything their website asked for. Demoralised and slightly embarrassed, I trudged back past the 30 people who now made up the queue.

To my relief there was an internet cafe just around the corner, which was clearly used to helping people with visas. Here I paid £4 and had the correct paperwork filled out for me. On my return to the visa office 15 minutes later, the queue had gone down considerably, so I did not actually have to wait too long to be served once more. This time, when I made it to the front of the queue, the clerk was happy to take my documents from me and said I did not need an appointment (which saved me a lot of time) and that I should come back in five working days' time.

I was fairly pleased, as the bureaucratic ordeal of procuring a visa is never straight forward or pleasant, but it did mean I would not get the visa as soon as I would have liked or expected. I had read that it was five days return, which is vastly different to five working days, especially as they are not open on Wednesdays. This meant it would be ready to pick up in a week and I consequently would not have enough time to explore Uzbekistan beyond Tashkent, the capital. I decided I would return to the embassy on Tuesday, hoping they would have completed the process and that I could pick up my visa. Until then I had a few days to kill.

With more free time than anticipated, but still in possession of my passport, I went to Kyrgyzstan for a couple of days and explored Turkistan and the hugely impressive Yasaui Mausoleum and the surrounding cluster of buildings. I also rode on over a dozen buses and spent hours walking, before it was eventually time to go back to the Uzbekistan embassy.

I had my fingers crossed as I waited in line. An embassy worker came out and addressed the crowd; a man who spoke Russian (it is very similar to Kazakh) translated for us tourists. Everyone who required an Uzbek visa was called forward first. Once inside the consulate, we all handed over our passports and then over an hour later the man who had taken them came out and started reading names and handing out billing slips (you had to take these to the bank around the corner and pay $75 and return with another slip of paper). Straight away I was a little dubious, as I could see a maroon coloured passport[17] in his hand, separated from the main pile of passports. I knew I was not meant to be getting a visa until Thursday, so I did not get my hopes up. Presuming that was my passport, I was in the same boat as someone else, because there was also a blue (American) passport on top of the maroon one in the separate pile of two.

After all the names had been called there was just my passport and a middle-aged American's, who I had coincidentally been chatting to whilst we waited. We were asked if we had submitted an application (which we both had last week; the American had actually done his five working days ago, a full week before). We then had to wait a further 40 minutes whilst the man went away to look for our applications. He eventually came back and gave us the crippling blow of saying we had to come back in two days' time, on Thursday. There was no margin for negotiations and no "extra payment for quick processing" (it is always worth asking).

Having been at the embassy for over three hours, I was in dire need of a drink. So I found a café with Wi-Fi and started to plan again, looking at alternative ways of getting to Uzbekistan (now

---

[17] All countries who are members of the European Union have maroon coloured passports.

with a shorter time frame) and at getting home. At that moment it looked like I might have to buy a new flight home from Almaty, try and get a refund from Tashkent (Uzbekistan's capital) and return to visit Uzbekistan properly another time in the future.

In addition to my struggle with the procurement of an Uzbek visa, there is a law in Kazakhstan that says if you wish to stay five or more days you have to register. Although, like a lot of things in Central Asia, it was not the easiest solution, as the registration office was only open limited hours on specific days. It was also meant to be free, but travellers were often charged a "registration fee". Wanting to avoid queuing and potentially not even being able to register, I decided to leave the country.

I do not have anything against Kazakhstan, just the registration process for tourists. Sitting on a bus to Kyrgyzstan and back whilst reading my book sounded like a much better use of my time; certainly better than hanging around more government offices and struggling with the never-ending bureaucracy.

I caught a city bus to the long-distance bus station, bought a ticket to Bishkek and settled down in my seat. I had to wait at least half an hour before the bus was full and we could leave.

After we had finally set off it then took around three hours to get to the border, which was quite straight forward, but still took an hour to clear the crossing. Half an hour of driving on the other side we arrived in the Kyrgyz capital.

At Bishkek bus terminal, my halfway point, I bought a drink, a packet of crisps and a return ticket to Almaty. Again I had to wait ages for the bus to fill up and even when there were no more spare seats we did not leave for another 10 minutes or so. Eventually we were back on the road, but it was already mid-afternoon by now. I put in my headphones and watched the sun dip toward the horizon. I was very happy with my choice to leave the country and return, instead of spending the day in an office procuring a registration stamp.

Back at the border there was a slightly longer wait to cross, but in total it was only about an hour. On the journey from the border to Almaty we followed the line of mountains again and I was able to watch an impressive sunset before getting to the outskirts of the city in darkness.

The following day was visa collection day. I packed my bag and walked the 35 minutes across town to the Uzbekistan Embassy and arrived on the dot of three. Five minutes later they opened up and called forward those requiring visas. Collectively we handed over our passports and began the wait; an hour and a half later the consul came out with payments slips to be taken to the bank. Thankfully my name was the first one he read out, so I sped away to the bank and was able to pay in a matter of minutes; others had to wait at least half an hour. I dashed back (vainly hoping I would be issued a visa straight away) and on handing over my 'proof of payment voucher' was told to come back in an hour.

To while away the time, I bought some pastries for dinner and had an iced coffee (to make use of the coffee shop's Wi-Fi) and returned after 40 minutes. This turned out to be a shrewd move as my passport was available to be collected just five minutes later. By 17:30 I was out of the Embassy with a visa in my passport.

Straight away I jumped on a bus heading towards the bus station on the edge of the city. It took a whole hour to make the five-kilometre journey and once there I alighted, hoping all the spaces had not been filled to Shymkent (the closest city to the Uzbek border). I need not have worried as there were half a dozen coaches heading in that direction. I wandered around a couple of them trying in vain to work out when they were leaving. Unfortunately, nobody spoke any English, so after the fifth bus still did not know what I was trying to convey, I took the plunge and decided to go with them. It was a step up from other overnight buses I had been on, as with this one you received your own bed space, complete with pillow and blanket (a luxury). We also left five minutes after I got on, at 19:00, so a double bonus. The prospect of me making it to Uzbekistan in time for my flight had just taken a huge step in the right direction.

We stopped at about 20:30 briefly and also again at midnight. At the midnight stop every bus in Kazakhstan also appeared to be there. At least a dozen coaches had pulled in and disgorged their passengers. Not wanting to queue ages for the gents, I decided to find a dark area of scrub, off the parking area, away from everything (as I have done before). But just as I found somewhere suitable, a guy flashed a high-powered torch at me and then threw three rocks in my direction, whilst marching towards me and shouting in Kazakh. Not that I am in anyway a linguist, but I presumed you were not allowed to relieve yourself there. I ducked behind a bus and lost him in the shadows.

I arrived in Shymkent at 06:30 and almost immediately found a shared taxi to take me to the border crossing. It took just over two hours and cost me roughly £4. When we arrived at the border the woman who drove us started asking for more money than we had agreed on. I deployed the "I do not understand what you are saying" card, extricated myself from the vehicle and walked away. I was tired and not in the mood to be hustled.

There was a short queue on the Kazakh side and I was quickly stamped out of the country. This was a triumphal moment for me as I had officially filled up a passport; a feat that had taken me four and a half years and a journey through 67 countries to complete. I hoped the next one would be filled more quickly. On the Uzbekistan side there was a large queue, which moved slowly, but eventually I was allowed in, with my visa being marked with an orange stamp. We then filled out customs declarations, which were taken off us, (more on that later) and then I was free to go.

Having had such a fiasco with my Uzbek visa I now only had a day in the country before flying home. Not wanting to waste any of it, I travelled to Tashkent, checked into my hostel and made plans for the day. I bumped into an Australian guy, who I had met at the Embassy (the second time I went), who showed me where to find the complimentary breakfast buffet and so we chatted over three servings of breakfast each (they were only small plates I promise), before I explored the capital.

Tashkent is quite a large city and with a population of five million, it is the largest in Central Asia and it shows. They have a subway system which is ornately decorated and worth riding on just to look at the stations. I also found the Presidential Palace, the Friday Mosque, Kulkedash Medressa and Chorus Bazaar, all of which I saw only briefly during my whistle-stop tour, trying to cram everything into my tight schedule. I returned to the hostel in the early afternoon to check in and have a shower (much needed). Once I had sorted my belongings I discovered the Russian Orthodox Cathedral, which was in a quiet park and had beautifully decorated domes.

The evening was spent with travellers from Germany and Austria. The three of us went in search of an attempt to break the Guinness World Record for the largest Plov (Uzbek national dish). By the time we arrived, however, it was over and the police were refusing entry into the arena where it was being held.

Later I had another shower, packed and went to bed just after 22:00. My sleep was short, as my alarm woke me at midnight. Having spent my (limited) local currency on dinner, I decided to walk the four kilometres to the airport, instead of getting a taxi, a luxury option not many cities have (certainly not in London).

When I arrived, just after one, I had to go through two security scanners before I had even entered the departures building. Inside I checked in quickly with Aeroflot - I was flying to London via Moscow. I also had to fill in a departure customs declaration. When I reached the (third) security scanner I was asked for the customs declaration and also my arrival one.

I had spoken to people at my hostel, so I was prepared for this, although when arriving I only thought you had to have one form. I had subsequently read that you are required to fill out two forms on arrival and keep one yourself. I had also read that people had been taken away for questioning and ended up bribing the security officials to be let through. Thankfully the guy I spoke to just said to "refill out the form, just make sure not to mention any money". I promptly did what I was told, returned to him and was allowed through to passport control without a hitch.

My mad dash finish across the Central Asian Steppe had ended. My flight left on time and I returned to London a few hours later, thankfully without the need to purchase a new plane ticket.

ETHIOPIAN PICKPOCKET

I had been wanting to visit Ethiopia for a long time. The main draw for me was the north of the country where they have some amazing stone churches, at a place called Lalibela. The churches have been carved out of the bed rock and are unique in their construction.

I also planned to tie in a trip to Somaliland, a self-declared independent state, which is still internationally recognised as part of Somalia. Somaliland is autonomous; it even has its own consulate in Whitechapel, London, where I was able to pick up a visa before I left. My motivation for visiting was the ancient cave paintings at Laas Geel, which are some of the oldest and best-preserved paintings anywhere in the world.

Setting off from London Heathrow I wondered how this trip would compare to my travels in West Africa. I have always been interested in diverse cultures, so I was looking forward to noticing any major cultural differences.

When I arrived in Addis Ababa, the capital of Ethiopia, I knew I would have the usual joy of trying to negotiate immigration and then once safe the other side, with my visa stamped, I would have to contend with the swarm of taxi drivers all shouting loudly, trying to gain my attention.

Once I had landed, after a long journey via Turkey, I found immigration to be fairly quick. As I had already worked out where I needed to go, I knew it was within walking distance of the airport, so I strode past the waiting drivers, into the hot, Ethiopian, evening air.

Exploring new cities at night is one of my favourite activities whilst travelling; many places come alive in the evening and their true characters are displayed. I also prefer walking to my accommodation after a flight, because it gives me an opportunity to stretch my legs after such a long time stationary. Addis Ababa was similar to many large African cities I had visited: hot, loud and vibrant. There was definitely a buzz to the place, as I wandered away from the airport.

Unfortunately I experienced my first personal encounter with theft whilst travelling shortly after leaving the airport. The threat came from a direction I had not anticipated and it was the one and only time (fingers crossed) that I have had an attempt made against me to steal any of my possessions. Its location took me by surprise as well considering I was on my way to a hostel, walking along a fairly busy thoroughfare and although it was late evening the street was well lit and there were dozens of people around.

I was wandering along, enjoying those tantalising initial impressions you have when visiting a country for the first time, trying to take in the whole experience, when two young boys, who were probably only seven or eight, started walking alongside me. I have found that this is quite a common occurrence throughout Africa, especially in countries where they have little interaction with white-skinned people.

The two boys tried their best to engage me in conversation, but I was thoroughly tired after a long day of travelling and just wanted to get into bed, so I said "hello" and carried on walking up the street, still attempting to take everything in as I went.

Clearly not put off by my lack of conversation, they followed me and continued to flank me as I walked on up the road, along uneven paving slabs which made up the pavement. Having not received the attention they were clearly after, one of them started poking in my side whilst the other boy showed me a magazine he was holding.

He asked if I wanted to buy it; again, not wanting to be rude, I politely declined his offer of purchasing the second-hand, second-rate publication. I had no idea what the magazine was actually about, but had no interest in it, especially as it was far from new. By this point I had started to feel pretty annoyed, as the other boy was still poking me in my side.

Frustrated and with a shorter temper than normal, I told them in no uncertain terms to "go away". Perhaps they struggled to understand what I said[18], or perhaps they were just not bothered that I was annoyed with them, but either way they continued to walk with me and with a dogged persistence they sustained their questioning and attempts to try and sell me the magazine. It was not until I stopped walking, raised my voice, glowered at each of them in turn and told them to get lost (a very British way of showing I was furious) that they eventually gave up and finally wandered away. I was somewhat relieved to see them heading away, down the road. I hoped they were going to bed and not to go and terrorise some other poor traveller fresh off a flight.

---

[18] The national language is Amharic although a lot of people are able to speak English.

As I continued walking along the road, out of a habit where I regularly check my valuables, I felt my pockets and noticed that both my trouser pocket zips had been tugged down about a third of the way (I always keep them zipped right up to the top when travelling, to stop things falling out). Thankfully they had not been pulled far enough down to enable the boys to get their small hands into my pockets and take my passport or phone which are always kept in there for ease of access and because I believe they are safer there than in my rucksack. The idea of losing either was not even worth considering.

I always try and be extremely careful not to display my money or camera when I walk around; only withdrawing enough cash to cover the next couple of days and just taking it out when I need it. Likewise I only display my camera to take pictures before returning it straight away into my satchel.

I was extremely thankful that firstly my trousers had zips and secondly that it was quite an old pair of trousers on which the zips did not slide freely. Had I been wearing another pair of trousers I am sure I would have lost my most valued possessions (at least they are when I am travelling). My trip could easily have been over before it had even started. It was not the most inviting welcome I have ever had to a country, but a lesson learnt that even small children can pose a threat.

However, my relief was short lived as when I made my way to the hostel where I planned to stay, I could not find it anywhere. I searched the immediate area and walked down dark alleys in a vain hope that I might come across the right building, but I had no luck. I struggled to see where it might be as the surrounding streets were predominantly low shack like buildings and in a rather down at heel neighbourhood.

Starting to despair, I even went into a couple of hotels in the broader vicinity and enquired if they knew the location of the hostel. When they had no idea of its location (or at least claimed not to know), I asked about the cost and availability of rooms in their establishments as a last gasp resort. It was approaching midnight in Ethiopia, but it was three in the morning in England, which is what my body clock was aligned to and I just wanted to sleep. However all the places were far too expensive for my meagre budget, so I carried on my wandering search.

I explored further afield from where the internet suggested the hostel should be and walked down even more unlikely streets. Eventually, after asking a shop owner, who called over a young man who spoke English, I found the answer I required. I was able to show the boy the name of my accommodation and he took me on a 10-minute walk to the place. Finally, I was there.

My troubles, however, were not over as to my dismay the hostel was fully booked. At this point I was ready to collapse into bed, so asked if I could just sleep on the sofa. I was leaving early the next day anyway to head north to Lalibela, so I would be up and gone before anyone else. Either through not understanding my intention, or not wanting a backpacker cluttering up his reception, I was refused the luxury of the sofa by the nightshift receptionist.

With patience running low I jumped on their WiFi and tried finding another suitable place nearby that would be within my inexpensive price range, especially as I was leaving early the next morning. I failed to locate anywhere suitable, so I resorted to my last option.

I had been given a parcel to deliver to a missionary couple, who lived in Addis Ababa, by a friend of my elder sister. I had their phone number in order to arrange meeting up to hand over the package (it felt slightly like some sort of dodgy deal). I am sure they were looking forward to their package of English tea and biscuits, but I am not sure they expected to be called at midnight to come and collect it.

After a brief conversation with Jasper, the husband, what proceeded was one of the most generous things I have ever experienced from a complete stranger. He decided the best course of action was for him to drive across the city (with two of his children) to pick me up and then allow me to stay at their house. By the time he got to me it was well after midnight and then the drive back across the city took nearly half an hour.

It was an excellent way to see more of the city and I was very grateful for the cup of tea, shower and mattress with which I was provided at such short notice - even though I spent most of the night being bitten by mosquitoes.

The following morning I was even dropped off at the airport, despite the early hour and they refused any payment for their generosity. I was truly grateful to the couple for taking in a complete stranger for the night. It turned out to be a very good end to a rather eventful first day in Ethiopia.

The rest of the trip saw me explore the impressive rock hewn churches at Lalibela before flying to Somalia. In the self-declared independent state of Somaliland (in northern Somalia) I was fortunate enough to be able to take a look at

Laas Geel which is a collection of caves, just over an hour from Hargeisa[19], that have paintings with an estimated age of 5000-11000 years old. A stunning collection of art which if the country was more stable would undoubtedly be a major African tourist attraction.

---

[19] The capital of Somaliland.

DEFYING DEATH IN THE HIMALAYAS

It was the first trip abroad I had ventured on by myself and I did not quite know what to expect. Over the years I had read so much in numerous books about Nepal and about the many large mountaineering expeditions to the Himalayas. I was excited beyond words to finally experience the world's most famous mountain range first-hand, but I was still slightly nervous about what lay ahead and how I would cope with the expedition itself.

After being waved goodbye at Heathrow (there were no tears as that was not our family's style), I checked in my mountaineering equipment, carried my tent as hand luggage, wore my expedition boots and down jacket through security and made my way to the gate. I found my seat on the plane, sat back and let my journey to Nepal begin.

I touched down in Kathmandu after a layover in Dubai, two delayed flights and a total of 27 hours travelling. On arrival, I joined the oversized queue for immigration, where my visa was stamped, and then walked through to baggage reclaim to join another equally long queue. Eventually, after waiting for all my kit for what seemed like ages, I made my way to the exit and out into the bustling capital of Nepal.

As soon as I stepped out of the terminal, I was mobbed by shouting taxi drivers all wanting my custom (and more importantly the money that came with it). Having listened to the advice given to me by a family friend, who used to live in Nepal, I had pre-booked a driver through my hotel to avoid having to deal with the melee. I shrugged them all off with many polite British "No thank yous" and tried to find my man, which was easier said than done in the crush of the crowd.

After weaving my way through the mass, as best as I could with three bags, I eventually found my driver who was holding a homemade placard with 'luck edward' scrawled across it. I presumed he meant me, so I walked with him to the car and hopped in.

Like the United Kingdom and neighbouring India, the Nepalis drive on the left-hand side of the road (a relic of the British Empire). Well, at least they are meant to; in practice, it appeared that as long as you did not crash, virtually anything else was acceptable. My initial observation was that it seemed that any speed or method of overtaking was allowed, with complete disregard for normal rules of the road. I found it ironic that the slogan 'slow drive, long life' was written on many vehicles. It made me wonder if the Hindu belief in reincarnation led to the reckless abandonment exhibited by most drivers. In addition, horns were used instead of mirrors, resulting in a cacophony of noise throughout the journey; a trend which continued throughout my entire trip.

The journey to the hotel was by no means a relaxing experience; the car was a low-slung sports car (with virtually no suspension) and the roads realistically required a four-wheel drive. The situation was not improved when my driver took it upon himself to drive down side streets in a vain attempt to avoid the traffic on the main roads. Instead of cars and vans we had to contend with cows, small children, piles of rubbish, hand carts, feral dogs and foot deep pot holes.

We arrived at the hotel, after what I can only describe as a traumatic experience. As soon as the car stopped, I clambered out, checking to make sure my spine was still in one piece. The walk up a couple of flights of stairs to my room got blood flowing again into my numb backside and once in my room I was happy to drop my bags and head straight out into Thamel, the tourist district of Kathmandu, for a much-needed drink and some food.

Thamel was a regular hangout during the Hippy-era, with many people ending their epic overland journeys in this part of Kathmandu. Today it has evolved into the tourist district of the city and is comprised of dozens of hotels, restaurants, outdoor shops and quirky cafes. Every other shop seemed to be an outdoor gear store, selling fake, knock-off items mainly im-ported from China. They sold everything that the intrepid adventurer or bargain hunting tourist might possibly need in the Himalayas. I found it a real assault on my senses whilst exploring, as there was noise and variety of smells all around. Coupled with the absence of rules on the roads, it looked like bedlam to me. However, secretly I loved it.

Whilst wandering along the narrow streets and back alleys, I found myself chatting to a number of the locals and became hooked by one particular man who was very persistent and was "keen to practice his English," (being young and naïve I knew no better). This man ended up taking me on a tour of Kathmandu, visiting Pashupatinath Temple and Boudhanath - the largest stupa in Nepal, revered as the holiest Tibetan Buddhist temple outside of Tibet. Thousands gather daily to make a kora, or ritual walk, around the perimeter of the dome. It was a thoroughly enjoyable day and I was able to see a great deal of the city, even if I got totally ripped off by the taxi driver who charged 4500 Rupees (roughly £35).

By the end of my first day in Nepal I had learnt the hard way to always agree on a price before starting a journey. I had also already started to fall in love with the country and preparations for my mountaineering expedition had begun.

The next three days were spent organising my trek. I had arranged to climb Mera Peak, which is 6,476 metres (21,247 ft) high and is one of the tallest 'trekking peaks' in Nepal. I had met my guide, a man called Assman (his name still makes me laugh), who was a rugged, dependable looking Nepali. He had grown up in the Himalayan foothills and had summitted Mera Peak over 25 times, so I felt I was in safe hands. To save money I would be carrying all of my own kit, which amounted to close on 30 kilograms. Assman would have a similarly large bag.

The big day quickly arrived and started when my alarm went off at 05:20, which left me enough time to get dressed and leave at quarter to six. At 05:40 I was already downstairs ready and waiting for Assman (although this was before I joined the Army, I have never liked being late). Assman had not turned up by 05:45 and after various phone calls by the hotel, at my panicked request, he finally arrived at 06:20. Normally I would say I am quite relaxed and laidback, but our flight was scheduled for departure 10 minutes after this and it was at least a 15-minute drive to the airport (traffic and crazy driving permitting). It seemed to me an impossible task to make the flight, but we set off for the airport regardless.

On arrival at the domestic terminal I saw that the plane had thankfully not yet left and it appeared to have no intention of doing so in the near future. The 'fog' (air pollution) grounded our flight until just after 10. Clearly it was something that occurred regularly and which Assman was aware of, but he had failed to pass this useful nugget of information onto me.

The flight itself was pretty dull up until the moment we had cleared the Kathmandu Valley and the mountains came into view. It was a truly stunning sight - only slightly ruined as I was repeatedly hit over the head by an SLR camera, being wielded by an overzealous Japanese man sitting behind me, who was trying to take pictures through the front window (it was only a small plane).

Mt. Everest (Sargamartha to the Nepalese) was just visible above the ridgeline, identifiable by its distinctive pyramid peak and then, as we rounded a corner, Lukla came into view, perched on the hillside, with its gravity defying airport. One of the most dangerous airports in the world due to its very short, uphill runway which ends at a cliff face, Lukla has claimed many lives over the years. So when we touched down and all the Japanese travellers started clapping at our safe landing (one of my biggest pet peeves) I nearly forgave them, as I myself breathed a sigh of relief.

Lukla is a reasonably well-established place. There are many bars and restaurants catering for foreign tastes, including two Irish bars (for a relatively small country the Irish seem to get everywhere). There was also a police station (nothing more than a glorified shed), a post office, two banks, a 'Starbucks Coffee', five snooker bars (I have no idea why there were so many) and my personal favourite, a YakDonalds.

After exploring Lukla, (it did not take long as there is only one street), I went and watched some football (apparently a major local tournament). I was underwhelmed by their skill and quite frankly English school children play better football. However, the lack of grass and prevalence of rocks on the dusty pitch is a challenge we are unaccustomed to.

As with most countries when there is money involved, there is a large dose of bureaucracy to accompany it. Expeditions in Nepal are certainly no different. After a lunch of momos (small vegetable dumplings with a spicy, chilli dipping sauce) we walked to the Lukla environment agency and tourist office in order to register our trek.

The office was meant to open at 09:00, but this being Nepal it was of course not open and Assman had to walk around knocking on doors, until he found the right man with the key. He eventually came and opened up at 10.30, but frustratingly did not have the authority to sign our form, so we had to wait another hour for his boss to arrive. Five hours after I awoke, we finally left Lukla with the required slip of paper, still with a massive day of trekking ahead of us. It was not the start we had hoped for.

143

Along all trekking routes in Nepal there are ubiquitous tea houses which serve tea (unsurprisingly) and a range of food dishes. Many of the tea houses have places to stay, varying from modernish en suites, to sleeping in one room around a fire with the owners. After 300m of ascent out of Lukla we had our first encounter with a tea house; we stopped and knocked on the door; with no reply we banged on all the doors in the small settlement, but nobody was there.

We walked on for another hour and climbed 200m before we had another break at another ghost town. At the third settlement there was still no sign of any human presence and by this point we also began to worry that there would be nobody further up the trail as a result of it being low season. If no tea houses were open, we would have no option but to cancel the expedition.

We decided to carry on up to the next high pass and hoped we could find some food. Luckily, a little higher up the trail, we bumped into four Nepalis on their way down. They gave us some hope as they told us that the owners of the next lodge had gone to visit a settlement over the col (a high pass between two mountains) but might be back that evening. It was a positive conversation, although not too reassuring as we had already passed our day's scheduled stop some time ago. With tired shoulders and legs, feeling very hungry and with diminishing water supplies we pressed on.

We arrived at the hut and could see five figures coming down the hill; we waited anxiously, hoping it was the owners. Thankfully it was them, but they had not intended to stop but continue down the hill to Lukla for the winter. They kindly took pity on us and left their eldest son in charge.

I do not want to say he was a lifesaver, but we could have been in a pretty ropey situation had he not stayed. We were very grateful and after three cups of tea we were feeling more refreshed and more like ourselves again. The altitude had made an impact on me and I had a mild headache which I could not shift. At altitudes over 2500m, the recommended height gain per day is to sleep at no more than 300m higher than the previous night, this allows your body to acclimatise to the reduced level of oxygen in the air. We had climbed over 1500m in desperation to find somewhere with food and shelter.

The plan for the following day was to double up and walk two days' worth of hiking in one epic trek, because nobody was at the high pass (4500m), where the next lodge was situated.

In the next valley we hoped to find another open tea house. So we left early at 07:00 and had a steep 300m climb to reach the first pass of the day, where we stopped to glug down some water which we had boiled that morning in the hut. However, on inspection of my bottle I saw that it was full of sediment. I mean it would have been more correctly described as sediment with dashes of water. You could not see from one side of my clear water bottle to the other, a result of filling up the bottles with boiled river water in the dark. I dread to think what our two meals of rice with dhal and many cups of tea would have looked like. I think it was maybe a good thing they did not have electricity and we could not see much by torch light.

During the morning we continued to climb and crossed two more passes, the highest of which was just shy of 5000m. On the other side we met a group of five coming the other way who told us they had summited Mera Peak four days previously. They said that they had been living off cereal bars and dried fruit for the past three days because none of the tea houses were occupied on their return; even the ones that were open on their way up were now shut. Assman and I walked a little bit further along the trail whilst discussing our options, but decided it was not worth the risk to carry on, so we turned around and headed back to Lukla.

It was extremely demoralising retracing the steps which we had worked so hard to climb over the last two days. This was especially true as I felt that all I had achieved was a throbbing headache, triggered by a combination of the altitude and dehydration I also had another sign of mild altitude sickness, severe wind, so I resigned myself to walking behind Assman. I did not blame him for the fact that he kept a steady distance in front of me during the entire decent. After a solid 12 hours of hard graft walking, we finally arrived back at Lukla, in the dark with our head torches on. It was one of the most exhausting days I have ever had as nine of those hours were spent well over 4000m.

That evening, over many cups of tea, we decided to change our plans and attempt to climb Island peak, the most popular 6000m mountain in the country. This plan, however, fell at the first hurdle because the Nepal Mountaineering Association (NMA) had booked the entire mountain to use for their annual climbing training and we were not allowed on it. We returned to the drawing board to think again. After some more tea we decided on climbing Lobouche East (6119m); a significantly harder, less well-known climb than either Mera or Island Peak. It is classed as PD+ (Peu Difficile plus) on the Alpine Grading System.

The following morning, we were back at the tourist office again to try and change the permit (in Nepal you need a different climbing permit for each individual peak you climb). Unfortunately for us it could not be changed, instead we were told we would have to buy a completely new one for $450, something I simply could not afford. Assman phoned his boss to see what he could do. He said he would ring the NMA on our behalf and try and sort something out.

The following day, having failed to obtain the permit through the NMA we decided to climb Lobouche East without a permit. Though technically illegal I felt morally justified as I had already paid for a permit which I was not going to use and Assman was happy as I was still paying him our agreed daily rate. Everything would be fine as long as we could talk our way through the handful of checkpoints along the route.

Just after lunch that day we had our first test when we got to a TIMS (mountaineering permit) checkpoint where Assman told the guard we were going to Everest Base Camp (Everest BC); I kept to the side and stayed silent. Basically, as long as nobody caught us on the mountain, we would not have to pay a $700 fine, something I definitely could not afford.

The next day was a huge struggle to get out of bed. The mornings had been getting progressively colder and colder the higher we journeyed. Personally, I think that there are few more uncomfortable feelings than getting out of the warm cocoon of a sleeping bag into sub-zero temperatures.

We wound our way onwards and upwards, ever closer to Everest. For an hour we ambled up a gentle gradient that took us to a cable bridge which swayed with every step you took across it. On the other side of the bridge, back on solid ground, it was steep uphill for over an hour. The majority of the time we were walking up steps, it was so steep.

The track eventually flattened out just before a police checkpoint; again, Assman fed them the same line about us going to Everest BC and again it worked and we were waved through. We had crossed another obstacle and we were one step closer to the mountain. Just past the check point was the famous hill village of Namche Bazaar, at an altitude of 3340m, the last major stepping stone before heading on towards Everest.

Two more days of plodding along the well-worn path to Everest BC were followed by a rest day. I had anticipated it was going to be a chilled out day of napping and hanging out with fellow mountaineers in the lodge, playing cards and drinking tea in the sun. Assman, however, had other things planned; his idea of a rest day was to climb a 5500m peak nearby.

By now snow was covering the ground and soon up to about a foot deep in some parts, but despite this it was a beautifully clear day with a vast expanse of blue sky stretched above us. The mountain we climbed was called Chhukung Ri, located a few hours walk away. On arrival at the base of the mountain, we made a fairly rapid ascent, having started from a relatively high altitude. Additionally we were travelling light with just two water bottles and some midget gems between us (the only equipment serious mountaineers need)[20].

Chhukung Ri was not a technically difficult climb, but it was a laborious ascent. Every time I stopped to catch my breath (which was frequently as we neared the summit) I was stunned by the majestic scenery which surrounded us. Mountains soared up in every direction and their

---

[20] Please do not use this as advice if you are undertaking an expedition more adventurous than walking to your nearest shop.

summits looked impossibly high. The sky was clear so we were able to see Makalu, Lhotse, Cho Oyu and Nuptse - mountains I had grown up reading about and on which some of my climbing heroes had made their name.

At the col just below the summit, and also on the peak itself, there were dozens of cairns in memory of the many mountaineers who had died on the surrounding mountains. It was a very humbling reminder that we were climbing in a dangerous area and that what we were going to undertake, in a couple of days-time, had a level of risk to it. After some obligatory summit pictures, we headed back down the mountain. At times we were actually running down the slope, trying not to slip in the snow. Seven hours after setting off we were back at the tea lodge. So much for a rest day.

We finally saw a glimpse of Lobouche East the next day, during a rather easy walk up the valley, the penultimate day before arriving at Lobouche BC. On first seeing the peak it appeared steeper than I had expected and certainly did not look like a walk in the park.

Just before dinner we walked up to a pass where there were again many memorials to people who had died on Everest and a few of the other neighbouring mountains; an additional humbling reminder of the dangers of high-altitude mountaineering. I have a note in my diary which I kept at the time and it simply says "The next two days are going to be big ones." I was not to be proved wrong.

With frozen water, boots and sun cream, (I only found out then that it was even possible for sun cream to freeze), we made the final trek to our base camp, which was situated high up next to a frozen lake. When we arrived, we cleared snow from a flat patch of ground and had the tent erected by midday.

Assman left me alone for four hours as he needed to go and set up a rope on what was supposedly a very difficult section. I offered to help, but he politely declined. This made me think and I wondered if he did not trust my climbing ability. In the mean time I boiled some water, ate some al dente rice (I was too lazy to wait) and drank some water, which took ages to organise as I had to melt copious amounts of snow just to make a little bit of water.

With some time to kill I wanted to enjoy the afternoon, so went off and had an awesome toilet trip. It had stunning views, arguably one of the most inspiring you would ever find. The side of the mountain dropped away, leaving a breath-taking panorama of the dozens of surrounding mountains. Later I tried to snatch some sleep, even though it was only the early afternoon, because I knew that in 13 hours we would be up and making our summit bid and I wanted to give myself the greatest possible chance of success.

Whilst lying there in my sleeping bag I thought I heard someone shouting, so I stuck my head out the door to listen and sure enough a cry and a whistle came from up the mountain. In a panic I struggled out of my sleeping bag, rammed my feet into my frozen boots, grabbed my discarded down jacket, gloves, hat and goggles and set off towards the sounds.

The shortest and quickest way towards the noise was up a rock face. 100 near vertical metres later, fuelled by adrenalin, I reached the top from where I could see most of the remaining route up the mountain. To my delight I spotted a figure moving upwards, which looked like Assman. Thankfully he was not in trouble and did not need rescuing, unlike my slumbering thoughts had suggested. I stood a little longer until my breathing settled - at that elevation I was higher than Mont Blanc and there was roughly half the amount of oxygen in the air compared with at sea level.

Whilst still trying to work out who had made the shouts I had heard, I scanned the mountain and noticed three other figures moving upwards; they again did not seem to be in any trouble. I was fairly annoyed that my efforts were wasted, but relieved that Assman and the other figures were all fine. But I was also confused as to where these other people had appeared from, as there had been no other steps in the snow ahead of us when we climbed to our base camp earlier that day.

I returned to the tent and eventually dropped off into a slumber again. This time I was only woken by the return of Assman; his arrival signified the start of snowfall. Whilst we were cooking noodles for dinner, he revealed that the shouts belonged to some Koreans who had just come up to have a look at Lobouche, but were not actually planning to climb it. This meant we would be the only people on the mountain for our summit attempt the following morning.

The snow must have stopped almost as soon as it started, because there was no noticeable coverage when we awoke. The alarm went off at 02:30, as we had intended to have a 03:00 start. An ambitious target even without allowing for "Assman time"[21] – he seemed to do everything impossibly slowly. We eventually left around 04.00.

---

[21] An additional period of time added to any activity as my guide was incapable of doing anything quickly.

The first two hours, before the sun came up, involved some of the sketchiest climbing I had ever done. We tip-toed across blank slabs of rock in snow covered boots, crossed icy sections of mountain and climbed gullies filled with scree or snow (or both on a couple of occasions) all with no ropes or helmets and just using a head torch to illuminate the way. Despite the conditions we made steady progress and I was lost in my own thoughts as we crept our way steadily up the mountain.

At first light, shortly after 06:00 we stopped to enjoy the sunrise as it slowly crept over the mountains, which was truly incredible. To this day it is one of the most amazing sights I have ever witnessed; just watching the first fingers of sunlight creep across the vast Himalayan expanse was spectacular, truly breath-taking.

Unfortunately, we could not stay there for-ever as it was well below freezing and we still had another 30 minutes of climbing to do before we were clear of the rock and needed to put on our crampons.

When we reached the edge of the rock band we sat down and started donning our crampons, well I say we, but only I put on my crampons whilst Assman attached his Yaktrak like contrap-tions (designed for walking on icy pavements, not for high altitude mountaineering; Google them). When I questioned his choice of equipment his reply was "it is only blue ice, it is easy", which quite frankly did not leave me feeling too confident. But then again, who was I to question this experienced mountaineer, who had grown up just down the valley?

We set off with ice axes in hand and hit the mountain, roped up via 10m of climbing rope. I had a sling harness (two slings larksfooted[22] together and joined by a karabiner); not something I wanted to fall on, but safe nonetheless. The reason for roping up was so we could easily place climbing gear as protection if it steepened or became much more technical. It would then mean that if one of us fell we would have a greater chance of stopping the other.

Together we moved fairly quickly up the mountain, zig zagging our way over the sastrugi[23]. It felt good; the excitement of reaching the summit was pushing my legs forward; the culmination of days of trekking, weeks of planning and many months of dreaming were nearing their final chapter. The sun was weak but it was starting to thaw out our cold bodies and was

---

[22] Also known as a Cow Hitch; it is a non-jamming knot used in climbing.

[23] Ridges of hard snow carved by the wind.

illuminating the magnificent peaks which surrounded us on every side. I had a massive grin on
my face and felt on top of the world.

After about 30 minutes of enjoyable climbing, which Assman was leading, he took a step
and suddenly his boot slipped and he fell. I had
been feeling the effects of the altitude, so was
taking a rest and had just looked up the mountain
in time to see him fall. It all happened so fast, but
I was able to brace myself in the arrest position,
ice axe embedded into the frozen snow with me
leaning my weight behind it.

Unfortunately for me, once Assman had
slipped 10m past me, his momentum ripped me
off the ice too. I saw a shower of snow kick up as
he slid past, gaining speed as he went. The slack
in the rope was almost immediately eaten up and
whipped around behind me; then came the sharp
yank as his momentum pulled the rope tight on
my harness and dragged me down the mountain
after him. Falling upside down, seeing nothing
but sky and shards of ice, I was being battered
about with no control over where I was heading,
I was just following Assman down the mountain.
I felt helpless.

After a brief disorientated pause, I regained
my senses and composed myself. I quickly realised the seriousness of the situation and flung out

my axe and thankfully managed to right myself, facing the mountain, and then immediately re-established my weight behind the axe with my grip firm on the shaft once again. I then watched in horror as the pick bounced off the ice in front of me, failing to gain purchase on the slope or to slow me down in any way at all. In my head I thought "this is not meant to be happening", as every time I had practiced in Scotland it always dug in easily. But to my dismay I kept sliding downwards and the pick continued to bounce off the rock hard sastrugi ice. I knew there was a cliff edge at the bottom of this slope, as we had walked past it not too long ago and I also knew we were sliding ever closer to it at an alarmingly fast speed. Eternity seemed to flash before me and I felt all hope was lost. My eyes were glued to the pick head, willing it to embed itself into the mountain, but despite having as much weight behind the axe as possible and being in a textbook ice axe arrest position we still continued to fall.

Nothing else in the world mattered to me in those few moments; my life was in my hands and I was not doing a great job at saving it. I wondered if this would be the end, perhaps my epitaph might say "Luke Edwards, he died doing what he loved"? It was possible that another cairn would be built for me at the bottom of the mountain and maybe I would just become another statistic for Himalayan mountaineering? Then, all of a sudden, I stopped. The roaring in my ears ceased, no more ice was being thrown up into my face and I was no longer being dragged over the ice. I could hardly believe it. The tip of my axe was resting on a ledge of ice, no more than one centimetre wide. I barely dared to breathe in case I upset the equilibrium and was sent flying downhill again.

Once we had stopped and whilst I was shaking violently from the adrenaline, I cautiously lifted one leg and kicked the prongs of my crampon into the ice to give me some additional security. I then followed it up with the other boot, blasting it into the mountain. This gave me peace of mind that I was not suddenly going to slip down again. I shifted my arms and flung my axe into the mountain face, providing another strong anchor. Now that I was in a secure position, I thought it a good idea to check on Assman. Carefully I elevated myself on my arms and peered down through the gap that I had made, between my body and the mountain, past my crampon clad boots. My eyes followed the rope down, as it snaked over the ice, to my climbing partner below. I saw him lying in the snow, not moving. I shouted down, hoping he was still alive and not injured, but there came no reply. Worried and not knowing what to do, images of 'Touching the Void' and having to cut the rope, like Simon Yates, flashed before my eyes. I tried to think of how I would sever the nylon threads as I had no knife on me. I wondered if my axe was up to the task.

Trying to assess the situation I glanced down again, and this time to my enormous relief, I saw Assman standing up, on a flatter part of the slope, seemingly unhurt. He saw I was looking at him and started making his way up to me. I was so relieved he was okay and that we had not fallen down over the cliff. Assman had stopped just 15m from the edge; he could easily have slipped over had I not brought us to a halt where I did. Whilst he was making his way up to me, I hacked out a small, flat space in the snow and sat down in it, still shaking slightly from the adrenaline overload. Never before had I come so close to death nor had I been so far from help. I hope I never experience that again.

As Assman climbed up he had a grin on his face and was holding his axe in one hand. He had feathers tumbling out of his down jacket where he had pierced it with his pick; they were caught in the wind and sent high into the thin Himalayan air.

When he got to me I asked my guide if he was ok to which he replied, "my axe wasn't working". I was surprised as this was not an answer to my question; I was a little taken aback. Actually, that is a lie. At the time I was really furious; not once did he offer a word of thanks for saving his life or apologise for his inadequacies as a mountaineer (let alone as a guide) to stop himself from falling.

I did not expect a medal or a bottle of Champagne (although it would have gone down nicely) but a slight show of gratitude would have been appreciated. If I had been unable to stop us, we would have plummeted down a 300m gully just 50 feet further down from where Assman stopped.

The closest he came to either thanking or apologising was to express that we "were very lucky". I will tell you what was very lucky, the fact I did not push him off that cliff myself. Of course, this was all internal dialogue and none of this anger was expressed to Assman, because that is not how the British conduct business. Instead I kept it all boiling inside and nodded my head in agreement that we had indeed been lucky.

Unsurprisingly the fall was easily the scariest thing that has ever happened to me and also one of the most painful. I can assure you that having two men's body weights pulling you down a rough icy surface for 70 metres takes its toll on you. It hurt to sit down and it was so painful to carry my rucksack as my hips were both badly bruised. My right elbow had also been heavily battered, so I could not put any weight on it. Aside from physical damage in the process of stopping over 20 stone, I managed to tear both my gloves due to the force exerted on the axe when trying to embed it in the ice.

After we had both recovered enough to continue, I untied myself from the rope, which still connected us, to prevent the same accident happening again and headed back up the mountain and on to the summit independently. I was so fuelled by adrenalin/rage I made it to the top first, beating Assman by about 15 minutes. We were both on the summit before 09:30 and spent almost 20 minutes on the top taking photos (you would not guess what had just happened by looking at them). Then we made our way off the top and back down.

I think I must have bashed my head pretty hard during the fall and suffered from short term memory loss, because Assman pulled a dodgy looking 200m rope from his bag and said it would be a quicker decent if I abseiled down. Two minutes later I was tied in and he was lowering me on it. It was very painful and I quickly realised I did not trust him at all, so it was not long before I untied and soloed the rest of the way down. I had had enough trouble with Assman being on the other end of the rope for one day already. We made a fairly rapid descent despite not using the rope and arrived back at base camp at 13:30.

We packed away the tent and the other camping equipment quickly and then we were off again, back down into the valley, heading lower with every step. Assman raced ahead of me, which was not that uncommon for him. But today he did not stop to let me catch up and have a break together; instead he just kept going, motoring along without a care in the world for me. I was trailing behind with a bruised back, rear, hips and leg, struggling with the weight of my bag after a mentally and physically exhausting day and there he was striding away like there was no tomorrow.

After a couple of hours of plodding along, at a slightly slower pace than normal, we came to a hill - the last obstacle of the day before we got to the village of Lobouche, where we were staying that night. When I saw the hill and noticed how far Assam was in front of me, I realised he had been racing ahead so he could go to the top, drop his pack, then come back and help me with mine.

This, however, was wishful thinking and my joy was short lived. As I got closer to the foot of the hill there was no sign of an Assman shaped figure descending from the top, so I walked doggedly on up the dirt path by myself. When I made it to the crest of the hill my elusive guide was just finishing his cigarette and I had been there no more than 30 seconds, just enough time to take off my rucksack, before he set off once again. No words past between us and we made our own way to the lodge. Only once we arrived did Assman say anything to me and again it was just to say how lucky we had been.

At this stage I was thoroughly frustrated with Assman so I decided that keeping my distance was probably not a bad idea. I introduced myself to three guys: an American called Max and a Dutch father and son, Bob and Jasper and spent the evening with them. We ended up playing cards and eating together, which was cool, although I wish there had been some beer available; it would have been greatly appreciated. When I regaled the events of the day, they were shocked and they too could not figure out Assman's attitude and strange behaviour.

The following day was a struggle. My alarm went off at 07:00, but I stayed in bed another half hour, because I knew that the owners were not early risers (we had stayed here a few days previously) and sure enough, once I had dressed and packed, they were still in bed. We eventually left about 08.30. The walking was pretty much a steady trot downhill to Dingboche, where Assman dropped off some climbing gear and picked up some clothes from a relative's house. This was a pleasant break and it was good to ease some of the pressure from my bruised body. After nearly an hour there we set off again.

At one point we had a small uphill section during which Assman stopped threequarters of the way up and asked if I wanted a break. I was managing the pain and coping fairly well, so said I was fine and that we should carry on. Not satisfied with this answer he then proceeded to ask if my feet and knees were ok because I was "getting very tired". I replied saying that the reason for me walking slower than normal was a result of my injuries picked up in the fall yesterday. Unsurprisingly this was met by silence and the conversation was dropped.

The awkward topic of the fall came up again a couple of more times throughout the day and again repeatedly I was told we were "very lucky". Thankfully the rest of the day was downhill or flat and was only interrupted by two or three short breaks. Along the track we passed a police checkpoint, but were just waved on through. The park officials were evidently more concerned with people entering the area with incorrect permits than they were with people leaving.

The tea house we stayed at that evening was owned by Assman's nephew, although he was in Kathmandu and when we arrived his nephew's wife was also out, bringing a horse from one of the neighbouring villages. So we waited an hour and a half for her to arrive. The wait was well worth it as we were treated to a lovely dinner of Dahl Bhat, one of my all-time favourite meals and the national dish of Nepal. Traditionally it consists of: rice (bhat), lentils (dahl), vegetables and a roti (unleavened bread). If you pay extra it will come with goat or chicken meat.

The room I was given had no curtains and my bed was right beside the window, so it meant I had an amazing view and could see Ama Dablam when I woke up (which was slightly earlier than I would have liked). Breakfast was an interesting experience to observe as we saw the process from start to finish: from the fire being lit with yak dung, through the melting and heating up of yak butter, more dung being added to the fire and then a batter mixture being cooked to make Tibetan pancakes. After many, many cups of tea we eventually left at round 10:00 as we only had a short walk to Namche Bazaar.

We arrived after just an hour and a half of walking, making it by far our shortest day yet, but even so the average for the previous three days was eight hours. I definitely welcomed the rest and although I do not want to lower the tone, the highlight of my day was the toilet. It was extremely nice to have a sit down, flush toilet rather than having to squat. It felt a long way from the 'toilet with a view' I had enjoyed at base camp just a couple of days previously.

A slow start the following day meant we left the lodge around 08:45. We had a quick browse around the market (which runs every Saturday) before heading off towards Lukla. At the market there was basically every type of produce you could imagine: huge tubs of butter were stacked next to jerry cans full of kerosene, shoes laid out on blue tarpaulin, spices piled high, sacks filled with potatoes and mounds of clothes that everyone felt the need to rummage through as they walked past. It really put western markets to shame.

As we left we had to pass through yet another police checkpoint, where Assman lied to the officer saying we had been walking the Chola Pass (a trek for which you do not need a permit). The other side of the booth was a steep descent with an undulating track which passed through a few more checkpoints and again the same lie was told. We only had two breaks during the whole day, but both of them were about 45 minutes long. At the first we bought tea and noodle soup and at the second we had more tea and a huge spring roll each. It was more the size and shape of a large Cornish pasty, but it was by far and away the nicest spring roll I had ever had.

On arriving in Lukla, eight hours after setting out from Namche, we went to the tourist office to obtain a letter which enabled me to get my $250 garbage deposit back. Not surprisingly the office was closed, so we visited the house of the lady who works there and she told us to return in 15 minutes. When we returned, she said to come back in an hour. At this point I had a distinct sense of déjà vu.

We passed the time at one of Assman's friend's tea shops, who made one of the nicest cups of coffee known to man (or at least it felt like it at the time). He frothed a small amount of some unknown substance (maybe yak milk) then added black coffee to fill the rest of the cup. We left there and visited another friend's place where we had some tea and Assman had some homemade 'wine'. I was given a glass to try and I have to say it was foul; not something I would recommend to anyone. I had not wanted to appear rude by leaving my wine, so I forced myself to drink some, then hurriedly washed the taste away with tea in an attempt to neutralise the disgusting flavour. The friend said it was not very strong, but I reckon it was about 30%+ and tasted like cheap vodka.

We were finally given the magic letter and returned to the lodge where we were staying. To my horror, when I sat down, I was given another celebratory glass of wine. I had no intention of drinking it, so as soon as Assman left the room I poured it into the pot plant behind where I was sitting (I hope it did not die from alcohol poisoning). Unfortunately, because I had drunk it so quickly, I was given another one...It was the worst drinking game I have ever played.

Flying back to Kathmandu turned out to be a similar story to our journey out to Lukla. After dressing and packing I was ready to leave and downstairs by 05:50. The previous night Assman had said 06:30 was when we needed to be ready, so this gave me plenty of time to have my breakfast. 06:30 came and went, so I asked the manager to go to Assman's room and check that he was awake; he was and at 7 he finally came down. Apparently I was on the second flight of the day, which did not fill me with much hope, as I had already heard four planes depart and land that morning. Assman was not joining me because he was returning to his village.

45 minutes later I had my ticket in hand, my bag had been checked in and I was through security and into the departure lounge, which was more like a roomy cupboard with a few broken seats. After 20 minutes waiting, we were herded like cattle outside. I am not really sure why, as we still waited over an hour and a half watching a further couple of dozen planes come and go before ours finally arrived (so much for the second plane).

This wait did however give me time to read plenty of the book I was ploughing through and also to study the police force. They really were not the most professional unit I had ever seen. The pilots were a different matter entirely, they all wore tight leather jackets and looked like they had just come off the set for Top Gun as extras as they strutted around. I was confused to where their arrogance came from as they were hardly flying fighter jets. Anyway, the lack of coffee that morning probably made me more critical and I am sure they were all very nice gentlemen.

We landed in Kathmandu at 10:45 and almost an hour later I was back at my hotel where I collected the belongings I had not taken on the trek. Three weeks after I had first arrived in Nepal I was back in Kathmandu, just about in one piece.

Later, after a period of contemplation, I spoke to an English missionary who told me that the explanation for Assman's behaviour after the accident was purely cultural. To admit that he had been in the wrong and it was his fault that the accident had occurred would have been the most embarrassing thing in his life. The reason he did not speak to me was because he was so ashamed.

Later I also looked at my insurance policy to see what had been covered if the accident turned out worse than it actually had. It transpired that the mountaineering insurance I had specifically bought to cover me for Mera Peak clearly stated that it did not cover Lobouche East, as it was deemed more dangerous. It is safe to say that I am very glad and thankful that the insurance was not needed and as my mum would say; "all's well that ended well."

PANAMA POLICE

Panama City was my last stop on an epic journey through Central America, which had started in Mexico and passed through every intervening country. Ever since I had read about the Panama Canal, in various school text books and numerous Guinness World Records books whilst growing up, I had been fascinated by the impressive feat of engineering; so I just had to go and see it. The canal is one of the largest in the world. When it was built at the start of the Twentieth Century, it cut the journey time for ships by weeks, as they no longer needed to go around Cape Horn and the tip of the South American continent.

I arrived in the capital in the early morning and went straight for a breakfast of pancakes and a coffee, before walking the not so direct route (thanks to the total lack of road signs) to the far side of the city, to Casco Viejo (the Old Quarter). Casco Viejo is where the expansion of Panama

City originally began, back when the canal was first being built.

The Old Quarter has, as you can imagine, plenty of Spanish colonial style buildings lining the narrow cobble stone streets; swanky hotels and restaurants were the dominant businesses and there were great views back across the bay to the city and the high-rise buildings which outlined the sky. I bought a mint choc chip ice cream and went in search of the world-famous channel of water.

At one point in time, whilst looking at various career options at school, I had wanted to be a civil engineer. Despite not going down that career path, bridges, buildings and feats of engineering still excite me.

It was not hard to find, due to its sheer scale. The canal is as wide as three London double-decker buses parked nose to tail and can accommodate ships the length of three football pitches. Reaching a place where I could take a picture without railings, trees or buildings in the way was slightly harder.

There was a museum dedicated to the canal at one of the locks, but that was about five kilometres away and quite frankly I could not be bothered to walk that distance and I was far too tight to pay for a taxi fare. Instead I opted for the classic backpacker transport and walked to the centre of a bridge to take my photo.

I spent a couple of moments judging the suitability of the bridge and the road which spanned it. The bridge was the American Bridge which is the main crossing point between Panama City and the north of the country (it turns out that it is a very major road). I also deduced that I was probably not allowed to walk across it. The main give away was that there was nobody else walking on the bridge, not a single person; no children or street dwellers ventured up and over the span. I am not naive enough to think that there just happened not to be anyone on the bridge at that moment; I knew you were not allowed to cross it on foot. In my head I reasoned that I would get away with it, i.e. I would just be able to say I was a tourist and was lost.

The walk to the centre of the bridge was an incredibly long trek (the bridge is over 1.6km long). Beforehand I had not appreciated how steep motorway bridges are, (they always look so flat), or how long they can be. In a car you just zoom over them and shoot down the other side in a couple of minutes; it takes substantially longer when walking.

As I made my way towards the centre of the bridge a number of cars flashed their lights or tooted their horns at me; I actually thought the first car to hoot me was being friendly, so I waved back. However, I quickly realised that they were trying to tell me I should not be there, but despite their warnings, I carried on regardless. I was somewhat stubborn and far too interested in taking that picture from the middle of the bridge to turn around.

Just as I was nearing the centre, I saw a police car shoot past with flashing lights and blaring horn. I desperately hoped they had not seen me behind the barrier and that they had more important business to attend to. When the driver slowed down in the centre lane and waited for a gap in the traffic to clear to enable him to turn the cop car around, I realised the game was up. I quickly took a handful of photos of both the bridge and the canal below. In no way were they award winning shots, however they serve as a lasting memory of the escapade.

Whilst I was still snapping away, I saw the blue lights out of the corner of my eye and heard the distinctive wail of the police siren. My heart sank and moments later the police car (it looked like a Ford Focus) pulled up alongside the railing where I was standing. A window was lowered and in no uncertain terms I was told to get into the white and blue car. I was shouted at in

Spanish, but despite not understanding the words being said, it did not take a linguist to work out what they meant.

Naturally I agreed to their shouting and gesticulating and clambered into the back seat, all the while wondering what sort of trouble I was in and where I was going to be taken. My immediate thought was that I was going to miss my flight back to the UK and I would have to buy a new one. There was also the potential worry of an awkward conversation with my boss explaining why I was not at work on Monday. To me this was a much more pressing issue than the thought of ending up in jail. I tried to think of what charge they could pin on me, jaywalking most probably.

By this point one of the cops had begun speaking to me, but my limited Spanish was so poor I could barely say that I did not understand him; I instead said it in English and told him I was British. In broken English he then told me I should not have been on the bridge; "thanks for clearing that up" I thought.

Once we had driven off the bridge, they pulled over at the side of the road and asked me where I needed to be dropped off. Not quite believing my luck and realising they did not want to charge me with jaywalking and that I was not going to end up in a Panamanian jail (thank God),

I decided it would be wise to vacate the vehicle as soon as possible, before they changed their mind.

I tried to tell them I wished to be dropped off in Casco Viejo, but perhaps my pronunciation was off, as they had no idea where it was; even when I showed them on a map on my phone they appeared to be flummoxed. Without knowing the name of anywhere else in the city, I asked if they could just leave me where we were. I was content and they seemed to be pleased to be rid of me, so after a handshake with one of the Police Officers and a parting "muchas gracias" from me, I was on my way, free once more.

Perhaps I should have thought slightly harder about where I was being dropped, as the neighbourhood I was now in would not have been found in any tourist brochure of the city. It might not even be found in some of the city's own publications as it looked rather forgotten and dilapidated. However, with no other option, I headed in the general direction of the Old Quarter and hoped I would get there in one piece. Almost immediately I began to walk along a street which clearly did not see tourists very regularly, if at all.

The street initially looked rather innocuous, but word had clearly quickly spread that there was a white man walking along it. Soon every doorway was filled with Latin American faces.

Trying desperately not to catch anyone's eye, but also attempting to keep my head held high, in an 'I am not afraid of you' type of way, I maintained an even pace and ran the gauntlet (at a steady stroll). All the while people appeared to be walking towards the road and I felt as if they were crowding in on me. I assessed the situation and reckoned I could out run some of the locals, as they were young or slightly tubby (or both). However there were undoubtedly a few kids who would be able to keep pace with me, or even chase me down, so I continued my nonchalant amble as if walking through a ghetto was something I did every day.

About half way along the street, with the end of the road and freedom in sight, there was a call of 'Blanco' hollered from behind me. I kept on walking, not wanting to show a reaction. In that brief moment I appreciated what it might be like for many oppressed people around the world. Here I was in a society very different from my own and I had been identified as being different by my skin colour. I was also offended that the man had called me Blanco, because I thought my tan was coming along quite nicely; maybe I was not as dark as a local, but I most certainly was not as pale as I had been on arrival.

Another minute or two and I would have been clear of the street; around the corner and I could relax once more. But just then I heard a can being kicked, an ominous sign from film and TV that you are being followed. Years of evolution screamed for me to turn around to look and see how close the predators were who were hunting me. I clenched my teeth in an attempt to fight my neck muscles from subconsciously engaging and turning my head. There were definitely people behind me, as I could hear their feet, but I could also see a road ahead, which was populated by people and cars. I was edging ever closer, all the while without being clobbered on the back of the head.

50 metres to go and I gave in to my fears and half turned my head to glance back. I saw a group of young men, in the middle of the street, running towards me. They were playing street football and had absolutely no interest in me (if they ever had in the first place). By this point I had made it to the end of the street without dying or getting mugged. The threat seemed very genuine at the time and to this day I still wonder if I was overreacting or if I had been in any sort of danger. It was certainly a very uncomfortable walk through an intimidating area.

ESCAPING ISRAEL

As with many of my trips, this one began at Heathrow. I was dropped off at the airport and sailed straight through security, as I had already checked in online. This journey was to be split between two locations: Lebanon and Israel and the Palestine Territories. There is no open land border between Lebanon and Israel, so I planned to fly between them; however, my first stop was Beirut.

I landed in the Lebanese capital at 03:15, roughly nine hours after departure. Frustratingly as I was seated towards the back of the plane, I was one of the last to disembark. But in traditional competitive spirit, I made sure to overtake plenty of people on the walk to passport control.

All my supporting documents for the visa (proof of residence, flight details out of Lebanon, contact details of Jonny - a family friend) were handed over collectively. However, the security guard took no notice of this carefully compiled stack of papers and instead just took his time thumbing through my (rather full) passport for an Israeli stamp. When he found no evidence of one, he issued my visa and sent me on my way; the whole process took no more than five minutes.

One of the main reasons for doing the trip in this order was the fact that many Arab countries refuse entry to anyone who has previously visited Israel - or at least has evidence of doing so in their passport. Lebanon is one of these countries. Israel has for many years assisted travellers by issuing a visa on a credit card sized piece of paper, which you do not have to stick in your passport, but I still did not wish to take the risk.

I was not able to check into my hostel until midday and did not fancy wandering around Beirut in the middle of the night, so I found a corner of the airport where there were some empty chairs, laid out and tried to sleep. Just after six in the morning I gave up and took a taxi into Hamra, one of Beirut's main districts, in which I would be staying.

My taxi driver pulled over at the side of the road and stopped for a coffee en route; not something you would catch a cabbie doing in London. However, he did invite me to join him and paid for my drink. The coffee was made by a little machine on the back of a handcart and came out strong and black; just the sort of drink you need to get the body firing on all cylinders early in the morning. I did regret it later, though, when I tried going to sleep.

When I arrived at my accommodation, I was still over six hours too early to check in, but after explaining my situation and saying that I had just come from the airport, the man on the front desk took pity on me and put me in their only available empty room. I then spent the next three hours half awake, half asleep in bed. Thanks caffeine.

Prior to flying to Lebanon, I had been in touch with my uncle's godson, Jonny, who worked in the capital for an NGO. After I had introduced myself via social media and assured him that I was not a creepy weirdo or a catfish[24], we agreed to meet in downtown Beirut for a mid-morning coffee.

Despite his recommendation to catch a taxi from my hotel to the café, as it was quite a distance, I decided to save myself the money and instead walk the two miles across the city. I always enjoy exploring a new city on foot, as I think

---

[24] Someone who pretends to be someone else on social media.

you acquire a greater understanding of the city, the street life and the general feel of the place.

I soon decided that I had made the correct choice. In a taxi I would have sailed past so many interesting sights; instead I was able to see remnants of the city's not too distant turbulent past.

Even though the civil war ended in 1990, there was still evidence of it on many buildings. This was particularly noticeable in more rundown areas, where the old office blocks remained pockmarked with bullet holes. There had been no obvious attempt to cover the damage or to repair them.

In contrast, downtown Beirut has completely changed in recent years. It has seen heavy investment and modernisation. You would never realise there had been any fighting. It seemed like it was part of a completely different city.

There was also a large military and armed police presence everywhere. This was predominantly a result of recent terrorist activity, although there was little threat in the north of the city (when I was there in 2016). Even so, imposing concrete barriers lined every street, designed to stop people parking at the side of the roads, in an attempt to prevent car bombs.

On top of this security, there were plenty of built up and barricaded Army sentry posts on road junctions. They had corrugated iron roofs and dozens of sandbags piled on top and in front of them. I think they were meant to reassure the civilian population; however, I found their presence slightly unnerving.

Jonny worked as a safety advisor for an NGO and when I visited he was advising on the forever changing situation in Syria, during the height of Daesh control. He himself narrowly escaped Syria when the fighting started in earnest. He told me he had caught a ride on the last UN convoy out of the country.

As you would expect of a man with his job, he was friendly and laid back, sporting an impressive beard. Over brunch and coffee we had a good long chat about loads of things, but I was most impressed by his resume of previous jobs (many of them in the Middle East). Despite having never met before, I learned that we actually had a friend in common back in the UK (a very small World).

As he had lived in the country for a couple of years, Jonny was also able to tell me about the city and the country, explaining how the current regional situation was affecting government policies and politics in general in Lebanon. All of this was super interesting, but most importantly he gave me recommendations for where to eat and what to see.

Buzzing from a caffeine overload and feeling the need to stretch my legs, I spent the afternoon exploring the city. I walked to the sea front and along the Corniche, which is a long promenade full of people running and cycling, as well as hundreds of pole fishermen all enjoying the sun. Quite a contrast to the bullet ridden parts of the city.

Trying not to get trapped in the throng, I made my way across the city. The walk took me past young boys screaming with delight whilst they jumped off rocks, past elegant beach clubs with their fancy pools, and along the sea defences to Pigeon Rocks, which are Beirut's famous natural offshore arches.

During my wanderings I walked through a southern district of the capital, which looked like a generic residential area, with apartment blocks and a handful of small shops. It was not until I saw the yellow and green of Hezbollah that I realised I probably should not have ventured this way. Houses, cars and mosques all flew the distinctive yellow flag, with a green arm outstretched, clutching an assault rifle.

Hezbollah has seats in parliament, fought against Daesh in Iraq and Syria and hates Al-

Qaeda. However, it is still considered a terrorist organisation by the United Kingdom and the United States of America, as well as multinational groups such as the European Union and the North Atlantic Treaty Organisation. I desperately hoped I would not be stopped and questioned or encounter any check points; being a British Army Officer probably would not go down too well. I calmly walked through the stronghold and breathed a sigh of relief when I could no longer see any yellow and green banners.

In the evening I went back downtown to see some of the old district at night, before heading to one of the restaurants Jonny recommended. Mediterranean food has always been one of my favourites and when you combine it with Middle Eastern style meat, it becomes a contender for the world's best food. I happily chomped my way through a huge meal of mezze, washed down with a couple of Almaza beers.

The meal was out of this world and consisted of: hummus (of course), kibbeh (croquettes of finely ground meat and minced onion encased in cracked wheat), labneh (thick yoghurt seasoned with olive oil and garlic), sambusas (fried cheese pastries), warak arish (stuffed vine leaves) and pitta bread. Suitably stuffed I left a large tip and went to my room to collapse in a food coma.

The next morning I set my alarm for the ridiculous hour of 05:30, taking the advice of Pegasus Airlines to arrive three hours before departure. This, in theory, left me with plenty of time to reach the airport, especially as I was unsure how to get there.

The airport was on the outskirts of the city; online there had been an article which described a junction where minivans parked and where you could hire one to the airport for just $2. Considering myself a canny explorer I was confident that I could find the junction, having convinced myself that my walk had taken me passed it yesterday. However, on arrival at said junction, there was no cluster of minibuses as I had expected, which meant nobody to take me to the airport.

In an optimistic moment I flagged a couple of passing ones down, but unsurprisingly they were not going in the right direction. The only bloke who offered me a ride wanted me to hire him as a private taxi, which would have cost at least 10 times as much; not something I was desperate enough for yet.

I walked downtown to see if there was anywhere there where I could catch a taxi. After searching around aimlessly a taxi driver pulled over and offered to take me for $6.50. I was tired and frustrated enough to accept the price of the fare.

We made it with plenty of time to spare, but before I could check in or go through to departures, I had to put all my belongings, including all hold luggage into a security scanner. For me this was slightly easier than for most people as I only had cabin baggage.

On the other side I went straight to security, as I had already checked in online and had a print out of my boarding pass. The security guard must have been in a bad mood, as he would not accept it, even though it had the correct barcode. Despite my pleas I was forced to join the queue at check in and wait to be issued a proper boarding card. Once through, I then had over two and a half hours to wait. I still have no idea why they said to be there so early.

The flight to Turkey[25] was like any other, although during the landing I thought we were going to tip over as we swerved violently to one side. I had a ticket for the second half of my journey to Israel; however, due to a stubborn lady when I checked in I did not have the boarding card to go with it. There was nowhere I could ask for help and have it printed out, so I had to buy a

---

[25] There are no direct flights from Lebanon to Israel.

visa for $30 and go through immigration, so I could enter Turkey. I did all of this just to go to the check in desk and print out a boarding pass to enable me to fly out a couple of hours later. A frustrating additional cost, which could easily have been avoided had the airline staff been friendlier and more sympathetic.

Once through passport control, I had four hours to wait for my flight to Antalya (my trip to Tel Aviv was in two parts). So like any good traveller, I found a coffee shop and opened my book. About an hour later some players from a Turkish football team arrived and invaded the space. Before long their constant noise made me gather together my belongings and go through to departures.

The flight to Antalya was delayed slightly, resulting in a number of us almost missing our onward connections. Thankfully we all made it in time, albeit a little hot after running between gates.

When we landed in Tel Aviv, the capital of Israel, it was late evening and there was still a queue at passport control. As I reached the desk the usual questions were asked: "Where are you staying?", "How long are you staying for?", "Who are you travelling with?" "Do you know anyone who lives here?" "Where have you flown from?" As well as: "Why did you go to Lebanon?", "What are you doing here?" After these questions I was 'interrogated' by yet another security official, off to one side, before I was finally given my visa card and allowed through.

A taxi was the quickest and by far the most efficient way to my hostel, but it was also the most expensive. Although I managed to knock the fare down considerably from what was initially asked, it was still pretty pricey. Nevertheless, the hostel where I was staying made up for it, as it was cheap, friendly and with a good backpacker vibe.

The next morning I left the hostel early and walked across the South of Tel Aviv to the Central Bus station, hoping to board one of the frequent services to Jerusalem. The terminal was a complete maze with no set structure, which meant I wandered around aimlessly until I eventually stumbled upon the correct desk. Here I bought a ticket and some snacks from a nearby kiosk.

On the drive itself we travelled past dozens of fields filled with grass scorched brown by the sun and countless olive groves, where you could make out all the little black fruit hanging from the branches. As we neared Jerusalem the countryside receded and the fields were slowly replaced with houses, becoming more built up with every kilometre and starting to look like any modern-day metropolis.

I had not booked accommodation, so on arrival in Jerusalem I took a tram to the centre of the city and chanced my luck at a hostel recommended in my guidebook. Thankfully they had a bed for me for the three nights I had anticipated staying. Although it was too early to check in, I was able to leave my bag at reception and head off exploring unencumbered.

Before arriving in Jerusalem, I had not realised the city was so distinctly split into two parts: the new city, which could be mistaken for any European city and the Old City which consists of four distinct districts (Muslim, Christian, Jewish and Armenian quarters). The Old City also contains all the major tourist sites, including the famous Temple Mount, which attracts pilgrims from all three religions[26].

I walked through the modern district towards the City Walls and the Jaffa Gate, which is at the top of the Old City by David's Tower. To visit Temple Mount I had to walk directly East through a number of long souks, endeavouring to

---

[26] Judaism, Christianity and Islam.

remain undistracted by items for sale. Eventually it opened up in a plaza with the impressive Western Wall along one edge. Whilst there I arranged to join a tour of the underground tunnels, which stretch from the Western Wall all the way underneath the city, following the remains of the wall along the way. However, it was not until later in the day, so for the couple of hours I had to kill, I continued to explore more of the Old City.

The tunnels were not quite the experience I had been expecting; geographically and structurally they were exactly as I had anticipated and I was suitably amazed, but the whole experience was ruined, or at least tarnished, by the tour guide. Firstly, I had no idea there was going to be a guide. I had presumed we would be able to explore the tunnels at our leisure. Clearly this was not the case, but worse still, the guide would not stop talking. There is information and there is information overload and she was definitely in the latter category. We were also constantly waiting for people to catch up and when they finally did, they invariably asked lots of questions. One positive that I took away from the experience was that it completely cemented my dislike for tour guides and confirmed my love of self-exploration.

Needing to blow off some steam and requiring some fresh air, I walked out of the city and headed east to the foot of the Mount of Olives. Once there I entered the Garden of Gethsemane, which was considerably quieter than the centre of Jerusalem. Despite the passing of nearly 2000 years I could see why Jesus often went there to escape the hubbub of the city. After this I climbed to the top of the Mount of Olives giving me amazing views back to the Old City, with the Dome of the Rock clearly visible on the skyline. At the foot of the hill I saw the tomb of the Virgin Mary,[27] which was too much like a shrine for my liking; full of incense, candles and effigies.

Back at the hostel I showered and changed before going out in search of food. After about 20 minutes I had still not found anywhere suitable, so I went to a kebab shop. When I had passed it earlier it was full of locals (never a bad sign) and proceeded to have one of the best kebabs I have ever eaten (certainly in my top five).

The following morning my alarm went off at 06:00, as I had the best intentions of visiting The Temple Mount as soon as it opened. But as I still had plenty of time in Jerusalem, I turned over and went back to sleep. The promise of a free break-

---

[27] Mary the Mother of Jesus

fast finally coaxed me up at 08:00; a couple of slices of toast and a cup of tea set me up for the day.

A tram ride later and I was back at the central bus station, queuing for a ticket to take me to Ein Gedi, one of the settlements along the shore of the Dead Sea. I jumped off at one of the stops, as I knew that along that part of the Dead Sea coast there were three hotels just a little bit further south (one, three and six kilometres away). I started walking along the road, hoping to find one with a beach where I could while away some time.

I really should have done more research, as neither of the first two were on the correct side of the road to have a beach front and nor did the third, when I eventually reached it. From that hotel I could see, in the distance, what looked like another hotel and what appeared to be people by the sea, but at a couple of kilometres distance they were nothing more than small shadows.

I took my chances and carried on walking, as I had nothing to lose. If it had turned out they were not people, there was nothing stopping me swimming anywhere I wanted other than the "Danger no swimming" signs every few hundred metres. Realising that I would have to pay to use the hotel's beach if I went through the front door,

I went cross country - striking out across the salt encrusted sand.

Again in hindsight this was not the wisest decision I have ever made, especially in flip flops. The terrain was a mix of soft mud and very hard, sharp salt crystals. Neither of these was particularly pleasant to walk on, especially in the blazing hot sun carrying a rucksack. I gained a new found respect for TE Lawrence, who spent much of his professional career in the Middle East and its many sandy quarters, and wondered how he managed to thrive in the harsh environment.

I eventually made it to the beach, which was indeed populated by people which justified my two-hour hike. It did not take me long to change into my swim shorts, as I was desperate to cool off in the salty water. The experience was truly unique. For some unknown reason I struggle to float in normal swimming pools, but at the lowest point on the surface of the earth, I had no trouble at all, due to the high salinity of the water.

After floating about for a while, I made the grave mistake of ducking my head under the water and came up with burning lips and the most painfully sore eyes I have ever had. It then dawned on me why nobody else was actually swimming.

I spent some time relaxing in the water before getting out and rinsing the salt water off. Despite nearly everyone else covering themselves in mud I did not fancy it, even if it was meant to be good for your skin. Lying in the sun was a good way to pass an hour, before going back into the water and taking the obligatory photograph of floating whilst reading a book.

Having once again dried in the sun I caught the shuttle 'bus' (a tractor pulling two carts) back up to the hotel. I then brazenly walked into the resort area and made a beeline straight for the pool. There I found an empty lounger and made myself at home.

A clear, clean pool was a refreshing change from the saltiness of the Dead Sea and a great way to spend the afternoon. On my way out of the resort, a couple of hours later, I realised it was actually a spa hotel. Catching a glimpse of the prices I saw that the cheapest package was over £100 and did not cover much more than the facilities I had used. I really had saved a great deal of money by walking all that way.

I caught a bus back to Jerusalem, where I found a small cafe where I read for a while. For dinner I strolled around and discovered a little place on the corner of some crossroads where I ordered a Georgie - a massive pulled pork sandwich with hummus and some incredible olives. It was a truly amazing sandwich especially accompanied by the glass of wine which I ordered. Apparently in Jerusalem a glass really means a glass (either that or they might have been trying to be edgy) so I received a tumbler of wine. Who knows? I might have been eating in Israel's response to Shoreditch. Since the sandwich was so good, I ordered it again, with another glass of wine. I left satisfied and felt I had received my money's worth, especially as I had not eaten any lunch.

I was determined to make it to The Temple Mount the following day, so I woke at six and made my way to the Moor's Gate (the only one through which non-Muslims are allowed to enter). On previous days the gate had opened at 07:00, so I arrived 15 minutes early to beat the queues. However, there was a handwritten sign telling me that the opening time was half seven that morning.

Not wanting to waste time I walked to the Church of the Holy Sepulchre, as I had not been able to see Jesus' tomb on my previous visit. There was a huge queue, so I skirted round a barrier to see if I could sneak in and take a look, but there was a dutiful priest standing on guard. He shouted at me and questioned why I was there; I had no decent answer, so made a hasty retreat back to the Moor's Gate where I joined a very short queue of eight people. Within 10 minutes this short queue had grown and there were over two hundred people behind me, nearly all from tour groups.

On Temple Mount itself the focal point is the famous temple in the centre, seen from many parts of the city. The Dome of the Rock stood out brightly with the morning sun reflecting off its golden roof. As I was first to it (other than a few Muslims milling around) I could take photos free from people and was able to walk around the whole Temple Mount unobstructed, exploring the different areas.

I returned to the hostel for breakfast and then made my way to the bus station to catch a bus to the Israeli/Palestinian border near Bethlehem. On the bus I chatted to an American girl who was studying in Israel and was visiting friends in Palestine. At the border the bus reached the end of the road and turned around (it was just a pedestrian border crossing). We made our way through the imposing concrete walls, which still separate the two countries, made famous by political artists using them as a canvas.

On the other side I asked two travellers if I could share a taxi with them to Bethlehem, as there were no buses on the Palestinian side (apart from tour buses). They agreed and we settled on a price with the driver. After haggling for a while, we decided on a short tour of the area, which included a couple of locations around Bethlehem. The price for each of us was just more than a single journey to Bethlehem, so we all felt it was a good deal.

Fernando, a Mexican teaching Spanish in Paris (who also spoke fluent English), was travelling with his mother (who spoke only Spanish) and they were my travel partners for two and a half hours in Palestine. Our first stop was the Shepherd's Fields. It was from here that the Shepherds were said to have been visited by angles and then gone to see baby Jesus.

The three of us were then driven to Manger Square in Bethlehem and joined the queue inside the Church of the Nativity. This was supposedly the place where Jesus was born (I took everything with a pinch of salt). After about half an hour we made it to the spot, which is indicated by a star on the floor, and fought our way to touch the star (or in some people's case, kiss it). Meanwhile tour guides, with large groups, tried to jostle you out of the way to get their customers in first. I was actually really disappointed and felt it was not worth the long wait in the queue for a very commercialised visit.

Our last stop in the 'tour' was the Milk Grotto Chapel, which was said to be where Mary fed Jesus on their way to Egypt; something I found hard to believe as it is just 200m away from the Church of the Nativity.

Palestine was very obviously a separate country to Israel. Aside from the massive concrete wall dividing the two nations, it was also the cultural and economic differences which stood out to me. Israel is an affluent country; its economy is on par with many European countries, whereas there is much poverty in Palestine. Simple things like roads and cleanliness are big economical markers and the fact that they do not have any public transport is also telling.

For a Palestinian to pass through into Israel they have to pay 2000 shekels (£400), which is about a month's wages and unattainable for most of the population. Personally, I cannot see the situation ever settling, because the Palestinians want Palestine to stretch from the river (River Jordan) to the sea (Mediterranean Sea). This would mean taking huge amounts of Israeli territory and Israel is unlikely to cede any land any time soon.

The rest of my day was spent having a late lunch, then exploring the City of David, just outside the Old City. There you could see the tomb of David and the room where the Last Supper was said to have been held. The tomb was not erected until the crusades, over 2000 years after King David's death, so there is some doubt over its authenticity. Nevertheless, it is still regarded as a Jewish holy place.

Later on, for dinner, I found a market which had restaurants and a couple of bars nestled amongst the food stalls. It was a perfect place to people watch.

On my final day in Israel I had a lazy start, but still left plenty of time to make it to the airport. I walked to the Sherut (shared taxi) rank, where I enquired about going to Tel Aviv airport. Minibuses to Tel Aviv are common, but nobody else was travelling to the airport at the same time. In the end I bartered for a price, which was considerably cheaper than the amount I paid on arrival. It also meant I used up all my remaining Shekels (Israeli currency), which was an added bonus.

I reached the airport four and a half hours before my flight was due. As I had already checked in online, I only needed to collect my boarding passes (I was flying Tel Aviv - Frankfurt

- London) before going through security. However, it turned out not to be quite that simple.

As a British passport holder (along with plenty of other nationalities) you have to go to a separate security desk to be asked questions about your stay; nothing too unusual about that. At the desk I was questioned about what I had been doing and more importantly (to the security guard at least) what had I been doing in Lebanon, Turkey and bizarrely Malaysia (I had a three-and-a-half-year-old stamp from there in my passport.)

I answered honestly that I had visited a friend in Beirut and had been there just one night. I had stayed in Turkey for six hours and only got a visa to enable me to get my boarding card printed and I had spent just 30 minutes in Malaysia, as I was just going over the border and back to extend my Thailand visa (Malaysia is not a country I count as having visited).To this day I do not know what I said wrong, but the security guard felt my answers were not good enough and he had to call his supervisor.

The lady who arrived asked many of the same questions about what I had been doing in Israel, as well as what I did back home. By this point in my life I had been in the Army for a couple of years, but I was also studying for a distance learning degree, so I produced my student ID and explained what I was studying. I also said that I worked part-time to pay for the trip, being vague about what I actually did. When she probed deeper, I replied saying that I worked in an outdoor shop, a job I had actually done as a teenager (I remember hearing someone say that it is always easier to lie about something that has some truth in it.)

Unfortunately, she was pretty smart and asked me why I was not at university, as it was term time. My brain worked wonders and I replied that it was reading week. However, she was quick to respond and asked where all the books were that I was using to study (the contents of my bag had been strewed about by another security guard), I shakily pointed to my Kindle and hoped she would not turn it on and demand to see them.

I was wondering where the questioning was leading and what I had done to be singled out. I was also very aware that I was treading a very thin line with my lies and could easily be tripped up at any point. About this time, she asked me if I had anything to hide as I looked nervous. Of course I was, because I had been questioned for nearly an hour and had still not got anywhere other than having my passport and boarding passes removed from me.

Yet again my answers were clearly not up to scratch, as she felt the need to get her boss, the head of airport security, to come and speak to me. He was at least more friendly than the previous two, but I felt as if my string of half-truths might come apart as he questioned Jonny's job and "how come you did not stay at his house?", "how long have you known him?" (I replied he was a family friend, better than replying I had met him for the first time in Beirut), "why had I travelled alone to Israel and how had I paid for it?"

After 15 more minutes of intense questioning, I was led to the security scanners. Here I had to take my flip flops off, empty the contents of my bag (my 75ml toothpaste was taken away as it was "too large") and I was taken to a changing room and searched (thankfully not invasively). Finally, after an hour and a half of searching and questions I was allowed to repack my bag, which had been strewed across five trays with every item swabbed for drugs and explosives.

Eventually I had everything back in order and wandered away from the security with a slight sigh of relief, although I was expecting to be called back any moment. It was not until I was sitting on the plane three hours later and when the aircraft's engines had started to roar and pull the plane forward that I relaxed, knowing that I was on my way home and not on my way to some prison under the suspicion of being a spy.

It was an experience which will always tar my memory of Israel. Even if the overwhelming crowds had not put me off returning, then the treatment I received at the airport certainly did. Coupled with the hatred they showed towards Palestine and Lebanon, I have certainly put the country at the bottom of my list of places to revisit.

Some people reading this might be wondering why I did not say I was in the Army right at the start. My answer is that I thought being a student would lead to fewer questions. The UK and Israel have a fairly good relationship with each other, so it probably would have been fine to mention my military connections, but in the moment I did not want to take the risk.

I think I was singled out because I was a solo traveller and not part of a package holiday, unlike ninety-nine percent of the tourists. If you then add into the mix the Lebanese visa stamps, I become a suspicious character in their eyes. However, I am still not convinced that these factors warranted an hour and a half interrogation.

THE CHICKEN THAT
CROSSED THE ROAD

After a couple of months on the road, travelling around South East Asia, I made my way to the backpacking capital of the world, Thailand. I travelled to the very north of the country to a town called Chiang Khong, which was right on the Laos border, only separated from its neighbour by the mighty, surging form of the Mekong River. I arrived at this rather sleepy town in the early evening and with not much else to do I skyped my family, who were holidaying back home in the UK, in the Lake District.

The following morning, I rolled over and eagerly turned off my first alarm and set it for an hour later, finally getting up at 07:45. The plan for my last day in Thailand was to hire a motorbike from the hostel and ride along one of the scenic mountain roads. Once I got my hands on the ubiquitous Honda 125cc, I filled the beauty up and rode away, pulling back on the throttle, the sun on my back and a full day of adventure ahead.

The proceeding 75km were spent racing along the flats and cruising through bends. The road was insanely good and with the sun shining, beautiful vistas around every bend and the road almost to myself, I struggled to think of a more enjoyable way to spend the day.

From Chiang Khong I rode south to a small town called Thoeng. Here I was able to turn to Chiang Kham, a road that was famed for its enjoyable riding (if you are struggling with the names you will be pleased to know that I did too at the time). It really was an unbelievable road; there were so many switchbacks dotted along its length, making me throw the bike into corners like a TT rider (at least it felt that way). At some points the road surface suddenly deteriorated and was pretty terrible. I was surprised, but extremely thankful, that I did not get a puncture. Unfortunately, though, the bike did not get off totally scot-free.

I was running out of petrol; the tank was nearly empty, so I was driving more conservatively than I had been. I came slowly down a treelined hill into a little village of bamboo huts, when out of absolutely nowhere a chicken ran into the road (I am sure there is a joke in there somewhere). Being the kind-hearted soul that I am and not wanting to hit the poor scraggly bird (as it would be worth a lot to the villager who owned it), I touched my breaks and swerved around the chicken. The road surface was slightly wet and my back wheel lost grip and slid the bike around, hitting the ground first on the right, then flipping onto the left, knocking the wing mirror off. I was fine, apart from a couple of very minor scratches and the bike likewise; or at least I thought so at the time. I continued down the hill, past some open fields and a couple of jackfruit trees and coasted into a town at the bottom, where I was able to fill up at the garage, where they had a handpump fuel station.

Whether in the chicken incident, or as a result of riding over the rough roads for a couple of hours or, most likely, a combination of the two, I noticed fuel leaking from the combustion chamber shortly after I had filled up. I continued riding, but half an hour later I had used a good two-thirds of a tank (a good proportion of which had sprayed onto my leg) so I pulled over at the next local mechanic I came across to get it fixed.

As I parked my bike three men approached inquisitively and asked in Thai what the issue was. Despite not having a word of the same language in common, they understood the gist of what I was saying. I think it helped that they could see where the fuel had leaked out. They ushered me into a grimy plastic seat whilst they undertook the repair task. It then took the three men nearly an hour to complete the job as they had to take off a couple of the panels to gain access and mend the broken bits; despite this, the work only cost me the equivalent of £2.20.

Initially when I rode off through the small village there were no drips, but unfortunately as soon as I filled up again there was leakage and fuel sprayed onto my foot once more. This time I had no idea where it was coming from or how to stop it and with no other real option available to me, I continued riding, hoping the bike would make it back in one piece.

When I arrived at my accommodation I was worried about what the owner would say about the state of the bike. He was holding my passport ransom as collateral against the bike and I had heard many horror stories of tourists damaging bikes in South East Asia and paying hundreds, sometimes thousands of pounds for repairs. To my relief, I received my passport back as he did not notice the occasional drip coming from the bottom of the bike. I went to my room feeling uneasy and hoped he would not notice the dripping or the minor damage to one of the panels and come banging on my door.

The next day I was up and awake by 07:00, enabling me to slip out quietly and not wake the owners. I was still concerned that I would have to pay for the damage. I could not see the bike outside when I left, so I was unable to check if it was still dripping; not that there was anything I could have done if it was, but I might have felt better is it had stopped.

Breakfast was bought on the way to the port and I was at passport control by 08:00. After a massive bowl of beef noodle soup (easily enough for two people), I was at the front of the queue ahead of opening time.

A long-tail boat was our mode of transport to cross the Mekong River and take me into Laos. The craft was a handmade, narrow, wooden boat with an engine on the back, linked up to a small propeller, which itself was on the end of a four-meter-long tiller. I had the pleasure of sharing the boat with three locals to cross the River. On the Laos side I was the first person off the boat and when I entered the gloomy, wooden Immigration Office and filled in my details, I was the first person that day to be issued a visa and to enter the country.

BRIBES AT THE BORDER

In my room in the Officers' Mess I was planning another trip to the West African coast. The journey took in three countries: Liberia, Sierra Leone and Guinea. Two of these I had failed to visit on a previous trip. I was researching a particularly interesting section of the route; a section which linked Robertsport in Liberia, across the border, to the Sierra Leone capital Freetown. This was a 489 kilometre stretch of my journey, which would be mainly on dirt roads threading their way through pristine rainforest. There was virtually no information online about the journey or how best to attempt it. The one account I read was of someone coming from the other direction, stopping at Bo, the last large town in Sierra Leone, 150 kilometres from the Liberian border. I decided I should allow at least two days to complete this epic journey.

A few weeks later I flew to West Africa via Morocco and began my trip by spending a couple of days in Monrovia, the capital of Liberia, exploring the city and eating dinner on the beach at sunset. I then decided it was time to head a little further along the coast to Robertsport. The town is small with few amenities, but is situated along a huge strip of pristine white sand beaches. The main (and arguably only) industry of the place is fishing, where the men still go out every day in handmade wooden boats and haul huge nets into shore by hand.

After a couple of days spent relaxing on the beach and exploring the town, I decided I would attempt to make the trip to Sierra Leone in one day. I had spoken to some people who said it was possible, if you set off at first light and realised that you would not arrive until the evening; that is if you made it at all. I liked the challenge, so planned to try the following morning.

I had set my alarm for 04:30, so when it went off, having packed the night before, I only needed to dress before I could leave, so I was on my way within five minutes. I had slept the night in a small tent on the beach, a little way from the edge of town, so the quickest way back to the centre of Robertsport was a 10-minute walk along the beach to the nearest road. There was something surreal about walking along a beach that has jungle on one side, the crashing sea on the other and overhead some of the clearest skies I had ever seen. The sun was not going to be up for another hour, so the stars were still bright and pierced through the black sky. Had I not had such a long day of travelling ahead of me, I would have been tempted to sit on the sand and stay for a while.

When I reached the road I brushed sand from my feet, put my shoes on and then using the torchlight on my phone, I walked the 45 minutes to the centre and the main junction out of town. Here I hoped to catch some transport towards the Sierra Leone border. Whilst walking, the only sounds I could hear were the crowing of cockerels and the quiet knocks and bangs of people beginning to wake up for the day.

An hour after my alarm had sounded, I was waiting at the junction in the dark. I was poised, ready to turn my torch on and flag down any early rising motorists. But before any vehicles passed me an 'Officer of the Town' approached and asked, "what are you doing?", which at 05:30 was a fair question and one I had already asked myself that morning. I told him my plan, to which he said nothing, but informed me there was a proper taxi rank, in the other direction of the junction. He then left and walked off towards it.

He presumably expected me to follow him, because he turned around and came back when he realised I had stayed where I was. He then made sure I came with him, showing me the proper taxi stop and even finding me a driver. I negotiated and settled on $25 to take me the two hours to the border. The price was more expensive than I would have liked, as I had hoped to share a ride with others, but it was certainly a huge time saver and we left immediately, so on balance I felt it was worth it.

We arrived at the border just before half-past seven, and after some toing and froing between the various desks, I was summoned into an office by a man who was sitting behind a desk in civilian clothing - not in uniform like all the other border guards. There was also a Sierra Leonean lady there, who was crossing back into her home country. We were both sceptical about his credentials, but followed him nonetheless. Eventually I was handed back my stamped passport and I could cross the border, over a bridge into Sierra Leone. During this five-minute walk I started talking to the lady, who was called Dora and I asked her advice about the most straightforward way to reach Freetown. It so happened that she was also heading there, so we agreed to share transport for the next stretch, once through immigration.

I have crossed dozens of land borders during my travels, most of them have been straight forward and the officials have generally been friendly and honest. It would be a lie to say the same for this crossing. I waited ages to receive my stamped passport (tourists went in a separate office to locals) and then I was ushered into a different office titled 'Health Office'. Once there, two men came in and inspected my Yellow Fever certificate. After a couple of excessively drawn out minutes the 'health officer' returned it to me and asked, "Where are your Cholera and Meningitis vaccinations?"

I was sure I had researched correctly and there was no requirement to have these vaccinations annotated on the Yellow Fever Certificate, but I was told otherwise by the officer. My heart dropped as he continued saying that I would have to return to Liberia and have them done there, wait six days, as an inoculation period, and then return. I immediately knew this was not an option as I had only been issued a single-entry visa for Liberia, for which I had just received an exit stamp. There was no way of going back and despite my explanations of having had two doses of Cholera vaccination already and that I had all the required Meningitis boosters as well, he was unwilling to back down. He undoubtedly knew I had few options.

I had my passport in my hand, so I was just about to leave and take my chances, when he explained that I would be turned away at the first check point I reached if I did not have the stamps in my booklet, so I was stuck. $40 was his asking fee to forge the signature and official stamp, backdating it to the required time ($40 is about a week's wage for a security officer). Despite thinking he was wrong, I had no other options. I was unwilling to take the risk of not having the stamp, so I reluctantly pulled out my wallet and handed over the cash. Significantly lighter in my pocket I re-joined Dora and had breakfast of rice with a spicy sauce, which is a standard meal for locals, but one I found odd for breakfast. Afterwards we went about finding a motorbike to transport us to Bo, the nearest town.

Our motorbike driver was a crazy local, who Dora knew as she had used him before. He made a huge song and dance about getting ready. Bo is the nearest town, but it is at the end of a very poor dirt track. The route is frequented by other vehicles; however it takes twice as long in a car as it does on a bike. Due to the poor conditions fine red dust is kicked up and covers everything.

Suitable precautions were needed before we departed. Firstly, our rucksacks were put into blue carrier bags before being strapped down and then our driver felt the need to put on some extra layers of clothing (I struggled to believe quite how many layers, especially as the temperature was 30 degrees). He put on two jumpers, a fleece jacket with a t-shirt over the top, two pairs of tracksuit trousers, over his current trousers and a pair of white wellies. I meanwhile was sweating in loose trousers and a t-shirt. I decided I would rather be dusty than sweaty.

The ride was an amazing experience; four hours of riding through the jungle, occasionally stopping at checkpoints (none of which checked my vaccinations). We broke down twice, which was sorted at the side of the road (replacing the sparkplugs and fixing some electronics); but otherwise we raced through tiny villages, watched snapshots of people's daily life unfold around us and at one point we stopped to wait for a small ferry to take us across a river.

It turned out to be one of the most enjoyable journeys I have made, despite being crammed on the bike with two other people and having very sore legs by the end. We arrived into a very hot and busy Bo just after midday. We washed our hands and faces of dust and then continued to the nearby bus station to start the next leg of the journey.

The stretch from Bo to Freetown should have been the easiest stretch, as it was all on metalled roads which should therefore have been quick and comfortable, but this was not the case. The minibus was originally built to take 15 people. However, with the addition of four seats in the aisle, the driver decided it would fit 25 people. This resulted in an extremely hot and sweaty ride for everyone on board; it also meant an increased strain on an old engine, which led to us continually breaking down. Even when we were moving and not at the side of the road, we were travelling at such a slow speed it was frustrating.

After yet another engine breakdown, where we stopped to get it fixed and endured an extended stop, we broke down again just 10 minutes up the road. This was the final straw, Dora and I decided to ditch the bus and flag down a different vehicle. It was already 18:00 and we should have arrived over an hour ago, but we were barely halfway. Luckily for us the first vehicle which stopped was a modern Toyota Landcruiser, whose occupants squeezed up to allow us in. Two hours later we were in the capital where I was dropped right outside the guesthouse where I was staying.

I had made it in a day, but I was exhausted. 16 hours of travelling, on some of the worst roads imaginable, without any air-conditioning, meant I stank and was still covered in a film of red dust from the motorcycle ride. The nine breakdowns were a hindrance, but they are all too readily expected and accepted as part of any journey in West Africa. The border was an uncomfortable situation, one I wished I had not found myself in, but the kindness showed by Dora far outweighed that negative experience. The journey through the jungle was also breath-taking and despite the hardships of the route, I would recommend it to anyone. If you can cope with the stress and being uncomfortable for such a length of time, I would also recommend completing the trip in one day. For me this choice meant an extra day on one of Sierra Leone's beaches, which was virtually deserted so I had it to myself.

A few days later on this trip I was on my way to Conakry Airport (by this point I had made my way to Guinea). I thought back to this memorable day and realised what a great experience it had been and one which was worth writing down. As I cleared immigration and settled down in a chair in the departures lounge,

I sat and wondered where in the world my next adventure would take me...

EPILOGUE

This collection of my escapades may well tell a story similar to that which some of you have experienced. However, for others, the tales may be foreign in every way. Whichever it is, I hope that all who have read the book have found pleasure in the retelling of my least enjoyable experiences around the world.

Travel is certainly not always the filtered version you frequently see on blogs and social media. I have visited plenty of the most 'photogenic' travel locations, but to achieve the right angle, lighting and for them to be free of people, takes either exceptional luck and timing or editing. I saw the Taj Mahal in India, with my girlfriend[28] and we have a picture of us standing

---

[28] During a recent adventure to Burma we spent a day exploring the temples at Bagan and during sunset, on an isolated temple, I proposed to her. I am sure there will be many more travel stories to tell in the coming years together. I am fortunate enough to have met the perfect travel companion.

in front of the tomb with nobody else in the frame. We woke at 4am and were the first people in the queue to be allowed in. We rushed to reach the spot, just to take this photo; the timing made it. However, I have also seen other people's photos, where they have edited people out to give their picture a completely different perspective. I hope that this book has made even a handful of people realise that not everything you see on social media is as pastel coloured and perfect as it may at first seem.

Finally I trust that this set of tales has been a catalyst for you to embark on your own adventures, whether they are small locally based ones or to the furthest reaches of this beautiful planet. May you be inspired to embark on your own escapades and to make your own stories.

ACKNOWLEDGEMENTS

My biggest thanks go to Harri Lewis and Nick Lowe, who accompanied me on some of my biggest escapades and helped me through some tough moments. Without them my travels would have been far less enjoyable. I am thankful that they share my passion for travel and adventure; the experiences we shared have undoubtedly brought us closer.

Without the sarcastic comments and helpful editing suggestions from Harri Lewis, this book may have taken a different form. My parents, Phil and Carol Edwards and close family friend, Julian Mills, also deserve a mention for their editing assistance.

I also wish to thank everyone who I ever met on the road, for making my travels so unique. There are so many people who are not mentioned in this book, some whose names I never even found out, but who helped me in some way or another; they are the people I will forever be indebted to.

My final thanks go to people like Dora, who assisted a complete stranger, to the people who went out for a drink with me after a tiring day and to those unlucky people who I have asked to take my photo, when I have been travelling solo. These are the people who add colour to travel and at the end of the day it is the human interactions which I remember most frequently and vividly.

CHRONOLOGY

The stories in this book have been group in a way the author believes reads well. They are separated into solo trips and shared trips. However there was a chronology to them which is listed below:

Defying Death in the Himalayas (2013)
Three Become One (2013)
The Chicken That Crossed The Road (2013)
Road Trip to Ruin (2015)
Flight From Hell (2016)
Panama Police (2016)
Escaping Israel (2016)
Riding The Ore Train (2016)
Guinea Visa Woes (2016)
Belts, Bullet Holes and Bandits (2017)
A Steppe Too Far (2017)
Ethiopian Pickpocket (2017)
Bribes At The Border (2018)

IG: @luke_w_edwards_

CPSIA information can be obtained
at www.ICGtesting.com
Printed in the USA
LVHW111528060919
630199LV00003B/480/P

9 781916 069121